Let me lead you through the chemo

a memoir

Jennifer Phillips

GradDipTh, BEd, DipIT, TTC, DipTchg

Title: Let me lead you through the chemo: a memoir
Author & Illustrator: Jennifer Kathleen Phillips
Artist: Jennifer Kathleen Phillips
Publisher: Wing To Wing
Mount Nathan, Queensland, Australia
Copyright: 2025 Jennifer Kathleen Phillips
ISBN: 978-1-7638719-0-8
Website: www.jenniferphillips.com.au

Other books by the author:
2018   Find The Ancient Path
2012   I want to travel with you
2012   Word Power Poetry and Poetics
2011   Israel Photographed
2004   You Can Make A Website
2000   © 2000 From New Zealand
1995   In Their Likeness
1992   In His Hands
1983   In His Time

Acknowledgements

I want to thank Pindara Hospital Doctors, Staff and Nurses, as well as my GP, friends, Genesis Church, family members and God. Your care made this difficult path not *too* difficult.

My husband Peter and sister Kathryn edited it, and our daughter Natalie did an assessment as well as two edits with me, which I appreciate greatly. Genesis Writing Group and friends also made suggestions for the text on the cover.

I pray that you will not only enjoy this memoir but be blessed with hope as you read it.

Bible verses are my translations, unless specified.

Some names have been changed to protect the privacy of medical staff. I have changed the name of my main Haematologist to Doctor Abba, meaning father, because he was so fatherly. His colleagues, I've called Doctor Paul and Doctor Sue. My General Practitioner I've abbreviated to GP.

Contents

The Hanging Baskets of Babylon were one of the seven wonders of the ancient world. One of the wonders of my world is the help I receive. It's like a multifaceted gem that sparks a rainbow of emotions like joyfulness. It is truly awesome in its timeliness and as refreshing as crystal clear water.

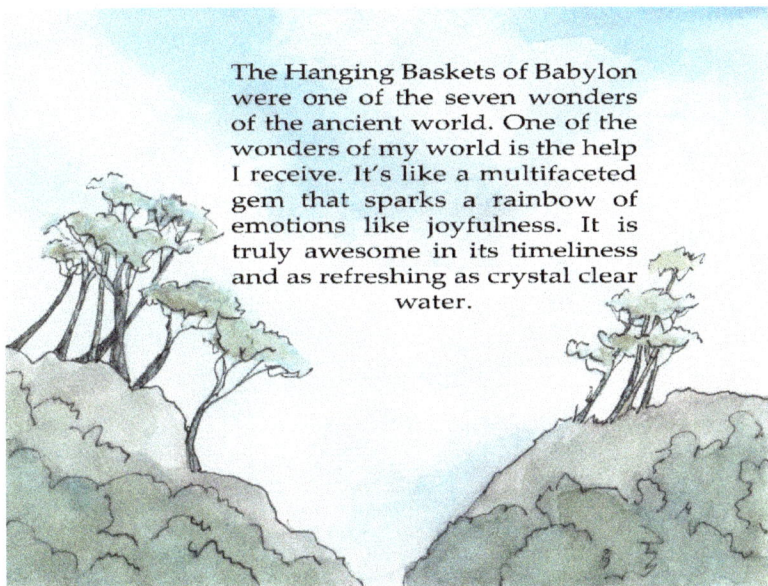

Chapter 1 ❧ That Was Strange

Watercolour and ink demo for Creative Hearts Art workshops in Australia Fair
(2020)

"If I give you anything stronger, you'll be a zombie," my GP said.

"I don't mind being a zombie. As long as it takes the pain away." I took a deep breath and said what I didn't want to say. "I can't live much longer like this."

Something wasn't right. I felt that. I'd noticed a significant deterioration in my memory around Christmas of 2020. Then, around March, I started getting a strange smell in my nose. It was a bit like the smell of moist leather on a hot horse. The smell reminded me of an unbearable smell I'd had in my nose after surgery in 2010. My jaw had been dislocated in a car accident in 2006. As a result, the bone had needed contouring, and the disc repositioned. It wasn't the first time I'd needed this surgery after a car accident. At the time I'd thought the smell was a reaction to Lansoprazole, a new tablet I'd been given for reflux. However, I discovered the reflux had been caused by another tablet I'd been taking for a severe lactose deficiency. So, I stopped taking the tablets. The reflux stopped but the smell didn't. I never thought to mention it to my GP. There were many things I forgot to tell

Me holding grandson, Harry

her. The unbearable pain in my hip, groin and leg swamped out other things.

I'd also been busy before the pain got to the unbearable stage. I was 67, married to my dear husband, Peter who was in his late 70's and was slowing down. He no longer spent much time outside working on our one and a half acres of land. Our property was enough to keep anyone busy regardless of their age. It could've kept me busy, but I was knitting for our first grandchild, holding art and craft workshops, making art, writing, maintaining websites and travelling ...

In April 2021 there had been a small window of opportunity to fly to Sydney before the borders closed due to Covid. Our first grandchild, Harry, had just been born and we couldn't wait to see, him. So, my husband Peter and I took the opportunity and flew down.

Harry was the beginning of the fulfilment of a word and vision the Lord had given me some years before. The word was about living to see my grandchildren. In the vision I'd been holding a baby boy in my hands and in front of him I saw the faint image of other babies down into the future.

How do *you* know what God is saying to you? One way I do, is through visions. This may sound strange to you if you have never had one or don't know people who do. However, it isn't

Mum and me having coffee at a café

something new. God spoke through visions in the past and let the ancient prophets know He was going to use visions and dreams to communicate to all kinds of people.[1] On the 27th March 2018 He'd let me know He was upgrading my "scope," and I began having dreams and visions in abundance.

I wanted to visit my elderly mother, but our visit to Sydney had depleted my finances. However, my mother said if I waited until June, it might be too late, so she paid for the trip. It turned out to be perfect timing.

While international travel was still limited because of Covid in 2021, there just happened to be a travel bubble between Australia and New Zealand at that time, so at last, I could visit my mother.

Everything was perfectly timed. If we'd gone to Sydney a few days later, I may not have been able to get out as they were taking people out of the queue when I checked in for my flight. I was asked when I'd been to Sydney. Thankfully,

[1] Joel 2:28

we'd returned a week before the cutoff date, so I was allowed on the plane, and thankfully again, I didn't have to go into quarantine when I arrived in New Zealand, nor did I catch a cold or Covid while flying over. I thought the mask must've worked. I'd forgotten I'd just had my first covid vaccination. Even though I had a severe headache and was very sleepy and tired for a week, I never thought the vaccination could've been the reason I didn't get Covid while travelling. I thought it was the mask.

While in New Zealand, I began taking an extra half a thyroid tablet as I didn't have time to visit my GP after the dermatologist had told me my thyroxine levels were down. It helped me feel a little less tired.

It was so lovely to be able to visit my mother as she went to heaven before I was well enough to visit her again.

When I returned to Australia, another blood test showed I was taking too much Thyroxin, so I was given a new script. I'd been having night-time sweats for some months, and they stopped. They stopped for two days. So, I looked up the symptoms of an underactive thyroid and discovered I had them, including increased sweating. I'd had an increase in sweating all summer but put it down to the heat. It wasn't summer now, but I was still sweating. I must have misread the symptoms because when I told my GP about the night sweats, she said night sweats usually came from an overactive thyroid, not an underactive one. That was strange.

Sometime in 2021 I began feeling hungrier than usual. So, for lunch I started having two slices of toast instead of one. I was delighted to discover I didn't put on any weight. I even lost a few kilos and felt great. I could eat anything now and didn't put on weight.

After a while of increased food intake, I thought it would be better to take advantage of this change and lose more weight, so I cut back to one slice of toast again. However, I was still eating more than I had before.

The next time I spoke to my GP, she said she didn't want me to go lower than 79 kilos. I was about the right weight for my height and age apparently. However, my

Paula and me at the opening of the Darcy Doyle exhibition

abdomen seemed to be growing. It had popped out. Surely, it should've shrunk with my weight loss. That was strange too.

I'd been holding art workshops at Australia Fair as part of the Creative Hearts Art co-operative. I was also holding card-making workshops with friends. However, I had trouble working out the change I needed to give to participants. Even as I was giving change, I couldn't remember who I'd given it to. Something wasn't right.

I no longer felt like being part of the Creative Hearts Art group. I was too tired even to gallery sit, which I loved doing. My motivation had gone. I struggled on for a while then gave it up. What was happening?

At the end of May I received an invitation to paint live at the Darcy Doyle awards exhibition in Mudgeeraba. The invitation said: "*You have been selected because we have reviewed your artwork and identified the high standard of work and interest to our community.*"

As I contemplated this invitation, it just seemed like too much work and stress. I declined it. I did however have enough strength to enter my latest artwork in the exhibition. I was so glad my friend Paula was able to drive me to the opening of the exhibition, as I didn't feel confident about driving there at night.

It was true. The pain down my legs was unbearable, much worse than the first time I'd been to see my GP about pain in the same area.

It was August 2021, and I'd just had my second guided cortisone injection into the greater trochanteric bursa (hip area). The strange thing was, that's not where the pain was. I'd finally worked out exactly where it was.

"The pain is in my groin and down my leg," I told my GP.

She leaned towards me full of kindness. "It will help whatever is going on in the area."

I nodded. I wanted to believe her.

I thought back to the first time I'd needed an injection in the same area. It had been April, earlier in the year. The leg pain had kept waking me up at night, so I'd asked my friends to pray for me. God answered our prayers, and the worst of the pain had just disappeared. I was still stiff though and found it hard to bend over.

At that time, I'd had a vision of two linear areas with pink around like inflammation. I immediately knew it was in my hip.

In April when I'd visited my GP, she sent me for an x-ray and ultrasound scan. The report that followed, mentioned a few things including possible mild bursitis. My GP suggested a guided cortisone injection. So, on Sunday at church I asked for prayer for the injection. When one of the ladies prayed, she too had a vision. It was of me as a deer leaping through the forest. The deer tripped on a log but got up and glided along. It sounded positive. I looked forward to gliding along.

A few days later, on the 8th April, I'd woken with no pain in the hip, only a bit in the lower back. I wasn't sure if I still needed the injection, so I asked the Lord.

"Go," I'd heard Him say, so I did.

I went to a specialist centre called Qscan. The radiologist had asked if I was allergic to anything. I was. I gave him a summary of what happened in hospital after I'd had jaw surgery in 2010. Back then, I'd been given an antihistamine injection because of the allergic reaction I had to morphine. After the surgery, I was very sleepy and nauseous. I was glad to sleep through the nausea, but my balance wasn't good, and I had trouble breathing. I would begin to doze off and suddenly I couldn't breathe. My chest was too tired. It was too much of an effort to get it to rise and fall. This usually jolted me awake but on one occasion, it didn't. At about four in the morning, I was outside my body looking down at it. I got such a shock when I realised it was my own body. It looked so ugly. My face was grey and blue around the mouth. My body was dead!

Suddenly I heard God proclaim the word *Wellbeing* to my dead body. I saw pinpricks of rainbow coloured light going into my face around where the surgeon had cut it. I watched as the colour began coming back into my face. Then I was back in my body looking out through my eyes and filled with great joy. I began praising God, along with a cloudy crowd above me.

I saw someone in my room. I thought she must be a cleaner. I told her what happened. The person left and two doctors came in, wanting to know what happened. Later a nurse said the cleaners were not there at four in the morning, so who was she?

The surgeon said the surgery went well. Subsequently, each time I went to visit he said, "Don't you scar?"

I looked at my foot. I had a scar there. "Yes," I replied.

On the third visit when the surgeon asked me the same question, I said, "I thought it was just your good surgery."

"No," he said. He looked puzzled.

I thought God must have done something special to my skin. No scarring? What a surprizing wonder!

I was allergic to some other medications as well, and before the injection I let the Qscan radiologist know. I also mentioned an unidentified rash. It was near where the injection was going. Each time I got the rash it had been worse than the time before. Now it had spread to another place on my tummy and back. It was extremely itchy. Because of that, I'd been referred to a dermatologist, on the 29th April and he'd done a biopsy. The biopsy report indicated the rash was a dermatological hypersensitivity, an allergic reaction from within, and not a skin-contact one. Following blood tests didn't add any further light to my condition, and none of the recommended creams had stopped the itch. The dermatologist did notice my thyroid levels were low. I was already taking thyroxine, so I needed to increase the dose. Was that why I'd been feeling so tired all year?

The rash wasn't a problem for the radiologist. I told him the pain in my hip had gone, and to check if I still needed the injection.

A doctor came into the room. "It's still a little bit inflamed," he said. "It's more diagnostic."

He used the ultrasound equipment to guide the cortisone injection into the hip bursa.

Afterwards, I wanted to understand the ultrasound image, so he showed me two inflamed linear areas that looked just like the vision I'd had. Then, pointing to the scan again he said, "The black area between the two linear areas shouldn't normally be there."

I wanted to ask more questions but didn't. Was the black area inflammation?

I remembered what my GP had said at the beginning of the year when I'd visited to find out the results of my regular diabetes blood test. "All the inflammation markers are up." That test result may have been the first indication that something wasn't right, but it didn't mean much to me at the time.

I couldn't live much longer like this.

On the 6th July 2021, I had a severe headache with left sided neck pain. I took some Panadol and fell into a deep sleep. When I woke my speech was momentarily slurry. I was very tired but never thought to do anything about it.

The following day during my regular card-making workshop with friends, I happened to mention it. One of the ladies had been a nurse and spoke quite sternly to me.

"You need to phone the doctor," she said. "I'm going to keep phoning you until you do."

"Okay, I'll do it right now," I said.

My GP wasn't available, but another was. He said I needed to go to the hospital. So, Peter took me to Pindara hospital.

I had a brain and neck scan and blood tests but nothing much showed up. I stayed in hospital overnight so more tests could be done. A neurologist visited me and said I may have had a small TIA (transient ischemic attack—small stroke), or a migraine. She'd seen an increase in migraines in some people after they'd had the Covid vaccination. I didn't think it was a migraine as I'd prayed for healing and hadn't had any since 1981. I'd had a few bad headaches but not ones where I needed to lie still in a dark room.

On the following Sunday, while in church, I had a sudden attack of pain in the head, so I asked for prayer. I was greatly encouraged and most of the pain went away.

I went to my GP for a follow up and she also thought the headache was probably a TIA, which wouldn't show up on the tests. She labelled it a *Funny episode*.

"Why call it funny?" I asked. "It wasn't."

"No," she said. "It's funny as in strange."

It was a *strange* episode and joined the list of other strange happenings.

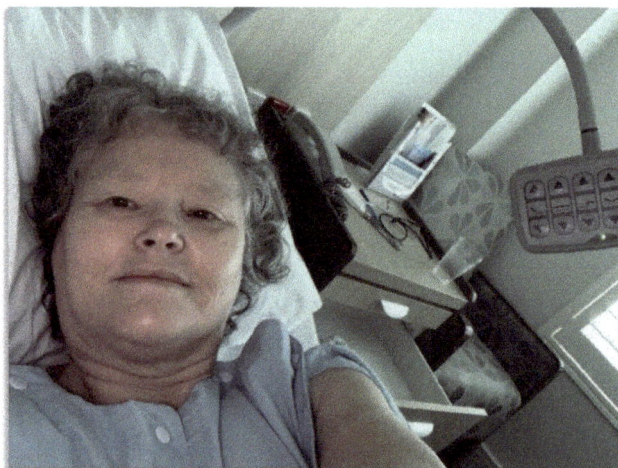

In Pindara hospital overnight following a "funny episode"

Chapter 2 ❧ A Zombie

Dancers (1970)

I seemed to be always visiting doctors for something. When I'd visited my GP on the 20th July. She asked how I was. I told her I was very tired and weary.

When I got home the Holy Spirit reminded me of the scripture, *"They that wait upon the Lord shall renew their vigour."*[2] So, I waited upon Him and the weariness lifted off.

I was back at the medical centre the following day for my second Covid vaccination. The day after that I heard the Lord say, *You are in my hand*. That meant my future was safe in Him. It was a word that was to have a greater impact and significance than it did at that time.

A week later I went to see a physiotherapist about my hip and leg pain. He suggested hot baths and gave me some

---

[2] Isaiah 40:31

exercises to do, like the movement that had brought on the first lot of groin pain in April.

The following day, after doing the exercises, the pain in my hip and groin was so strong I felt sick. I had some old codeine-based pain relief, so I tried it, but it didn't take all the pain away. I made another appointment with my GP. This time it was a teleconference.

"It will just take time," she said and gave me a referral for another ultra scan and a blood test. "Go back to the physiotherapist."

The blood test didn't show any blood clots, but some kind of infection.

When I went for the ultra-scan, inflammation was seen. The report noted some "*anterior labral changes*" and "*fluid in the greater tronchanteric bursa.*" So, the diagnosis was bursitis again.

That was when my GP sent me for the second guided cortisone injection. The injection didn't take all the pain away this time. I continued to try various codeine-based pain relief but had to stop them, as they were making me feel ill and strange in my head. I was allergic to morphine and some other pain relief, so what could I take?

I was sleeping my life away. Back to the doctor!

"Okay," my GP said, "We'll try immediate release Palexia."

We both hoped I wouldn't be allergic to Palexia.

I wasn't. That was so wonderful. We'd finally found something I could take for pain.

At home, we have a plaque on the wall with a Scripture verse from Proverbs 3:5-6 (Translation not specified).

Trust in the Lord with all your heart
lean not on your own understanding.

In all your ways acknowledge him,
and he will make your paths straight.

As I stood looking at it, I knew I should trust the Lord. He was always faithful, but my trust seemed to have become wobbly.

The Palexia did act fast, but the more I took, the shorter the pain relief was. In the end, one hour of pain relief wasn't long enough. So, I went back to my GP and begged for the sustained relief Palexia. That was when she said, "If I give you anything stronger, you'll be a zombie."

She wasn't keen to give it to me, but I had to try something.

I became the zombie I thought I wouldn't mind being, but I did mind. I hated it. I couldn't live like that either. I would just have to put up with pain sometimes.

I asked my church family and Facebook friends to pray again, and when they prayed, I was pain free, but it always came back. I needed prayer like daily bread.

I stopped the sustained release Palexia and used only Panadol and an occasional immediate release Palexia. I remembered the physiotherapist recommendation about hot baths and began having long hot baths before going to bed. They did help me get to sleep.

As I got into the bath one day, I saw a swelling on the left groin. That was strange. I could feel other lumps there too. I remembered what a doctor had said about 35 years before, when I'd had lumps on the opposite side.

"I don't know what they could be," he'd said, but didn't investigate.

I noticed after the car accident in 2006 that those lumps had disappeared. Maybe these would just disappear too.

The left side of my neck had a lump in it as well, and the muscles felt tight and sore. That was strange.

The car accident I'd had in 2006, had left me with a bulging disc in my neck. After eleven years, a man I'd never met before had prayed for me and said, among other things, the Lord was healing my right side. A few days later, I felt some clicks in my neck and the bulge disappeared. Sometime after that I'd been lying on my stomach and I'd heard an angel say, *"Roll over."*

I thought that was a strange thing for an angel to say, but I rolled over anyway. My head was shaken first to one side and then the other about a hundred miles an hour. After that I'd been able to lie comfortably on my right side for the first time in some years. I could also turn my head without pain. So, why had the neck pain come back?

I went for a neck massage. The lady massaged the lump away, and the muscles felt a little better.

The hip and groin pain were finally bearable, but the pain down my leg wasn't. Now I had pain down both legs and an occasional sharp jabbing pain on the right. Was my appendix inflamed? Was this what my life and my future was going to be? Was I about to die?

Around the end of July, in the misery of pain I sought God. "Where are you in all this?" They were not the words in my heart. I knew He was with me, and I knew the words were what other people said, but I whispered them in my mind. What I really meant was, "Help me, Lord. Please help me right now!"

God's reply was swift. *"Why is the blade song of the city moving through the church?"*

I didn't know what that meant.

Next, I heard the words, *"Shall we start death here?"*

"No," I said. Then I thought of continuing to live with the pain I had. I didn't want a painfully long and slow death. "Not unless I have a quick death," I added.

I felt as though this was what my life was going to be like from now on. Unbearable pain. If this cup could pass from me, I wanted it to. Cancer popped into my mind.

"No, not cancer." I rebuked even the thought of it. I didn't want that thought in my mind or my body either.

Some days or weeks later I thought I understood what God was saying. Even Christians were repeating the words of those around them and those that came via the media. The song of the city regarding Covid, wasn't the song God wanted us to sing. God wanted us to sing His song, the words He spoke to us individually.

While editing this book, I had a dream that explains this more clearly.

In the dream a man who represented a murderous spirit, attacked me with his blade. I got it off him and attacked him back with it. However, each time I used it on him it cut deeper into my own fingers.

The blade we are to use is the blade of the Spirit, commonly known as the Sword or dagger of the Spirit, which is the Word of God.[3] If each of us found out God's perspective of things for us, we could stand in the authority of what He says. No-one would need to judge another about what they did. One rule didn't fit all.

I needed to be honest with God and use the Lord's blade, the dagger of the Spirit too. I needed to use it against the hopelessness and fear that sometimes attacked me with the pain. I remembered the Bible verse, about life and death being set before people.[4] God wanted people to choose life. I wanted to die a quick death ... if I was dying. It felt like I

---

[3] Ephesians 6:17, (Litt, 1968)
[4] Deuteronomy 30:19

was. I didn't think I could cope with a long, drawn-out affair.

I remembered the last time I'd had unbearable hip pain. At the time, some of my church family thought I'd need a hip replacement. That was in 2017. In October that year, I was visiting our daughter Aimee in Sydney. Peter had given me money to buy a ruby necklace for our 40th wedding anniversary. So, we went shopping.

It wasn't long before I could hardly walk. "I have to sit down," I said.

We found a café. The wooden chair was aesthetically pleasing, but it wasn't comfortable. I began to feel miserable. I didn't think I could walk any more. Silently I cried out to God for help.

"You will improve," the Holy Spirit said.

"Yes. I will," I responded silently. I knew I would, but how long would it take?

Some of the pain immediately subsided and I was surprised. We were able to continue shopping. I was so joyful and thankful.

Not far from the café, we found a jeweller. There we found a lovely necklace. It was even on sale at half the normal price.

Now, as I thought about the dagger of the Spirit, a little hope pierced my dark thoughts. God *had* taken the pain away before. I yielded to Him.

"I choose life," I said. Regardless of what it would be like, I would follow that path.

"*I will help you,*" the Holy Spirit said, and He did. I rested in His word. It was the blade I needed ... and He did help me. He helped me through the night.

I woke at 3.30am drenched in sweat. I was so cold I had to change my night-clothes. I'd been having night sweats all year but hadn't thought much about it because it was summer. However, winter was a different story. I thought I would mention it to the doctor, but I kept forgetting.

The back of our property showing weeds on the bank

The next time I visited my GP I forgot to mention it again. The groin pain was upmost in my mind. I spoke of that and other things.

My GP looked at my latest blood tests and said, "I think it's the lymphatic system."

At home, I searched online for the lymphatic system, but what I read sounded too scary. Cancer ... I quickly closed the webpage. I wasn't that bad! I blocked it from my mind.

On the 16th of August, we got a phone call from a real estate agent. Someone was interested in buying our property. I didn't know how we'd get the house ready for a viewing. I was only managing a couple of little jobs around the house each day and was sleeping in the afternoon.

I thought it would take another year for us to finish the work that needed doing on and around our house. We had three jobs booked in with various trades people for August but decided to let the agent show the house anyway. If the price was right, we'd sell.

Maintaining one and a half acres was too much for me now. Peter had felt it was too much for him for some years. We hurriedly began preparing for the viewing. That night we searched the internet but couldn't find anything I liked on the market. I asked the Lord about selling our home.

"Wait," He said.

"Oh no! What can I do? I've said it's okay for someone to come through tomorrow. Please undertake for us."

The following morning the real estate agent phoned again and told us the people wanted to wait, as they didn't have their finances organised. I praised God! He had undertaken and prices were still going up. I told the agent about the house in our street that just sold. It didn't have the land, outbuildings and solar we had. He said he just looked at it and thought we could get $100K or so more than what he'd thought the day before. I relaxed. I was supposed to be taking it easy anyway.

"Give us a call in a month's time," I said. The jobs we'd booked in would be completed by then—or so I thought!

Chapter 3 ◈ Angel Wings

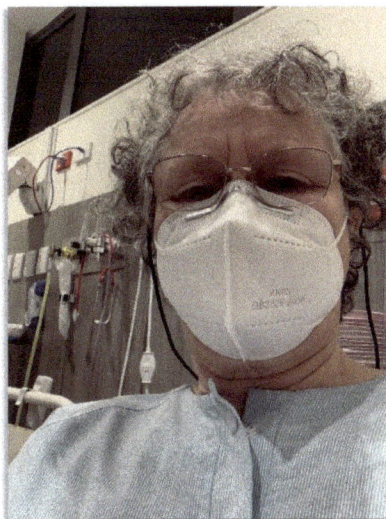

A quick selfie at Pindara Private Hospital

Not only did both my legs ache badly all night, but my throat felt thick. I also had abdominal pains. The following day, Friday the 27th August, I woke with bowel trouble. I made at least 8 trips to the toilet. I wasn't sure if I'd be well enough to go to our normal morning tea appointment with friends, but things settled, so I took the risk. I was fine. It was a good diversion from the pain.

In the afternoon I was very tired, but I needed to prune some of the Lilli Pilli trees. The people we had booked to do various gardening tasks had failed to come. I'd booked someone to dig holes along the bank for four magnolia trees I'd bought. We'd also booked a garden maintenance man with goats to clear the bank. The work was still waiting to be done. Someone had to do it. I decided that someone would just have to be me.

I got the chainsaw out and felled the branches. Only I felled myself as well! I just fell over on my side. I expected a hard landing, but it was so soft. It felt like I'd landed on angel wings. That was strange. I got a fright when I saw I was still holding the chainsaw with both hands outstretched. Thankfully the chainsaw had stopped, even with both hands on it. I slapped the branches I'd landed on to see if they were really that soft. Maybe I *had* landed on angel wings.

I felt washed out. I had no energy to saw another branch, so I stopped what I was doing.

Suddenly I got chills, and my teeth started chattering. I didn't feel well. There was a lump in my throat again. I wondered if I had Covid. I was shivering so much I put a thick coat on. I tried to make a doctor's appointment, but they were all booked out. The receptionist suggested phoning the health line. I didn't. Instead, I pressured Peter to take me for a Covid test. I didn't feel well enough to drive myself.

Peter drove me into Nerang where we discovered all the Covid testing stations were closed because it was a public holiday.

Back home, I stopped shivering under my thick coat, but my head felt hot. I hunted for a thermometer and found one. My temperature was just over 37.8 Celsius. Then it went up to 38.4.

I searched online to find out about temperature ranges and discovered anything over 38 was a fever. I phoned the health line. The lady I spoke to asked me many medical history questions. I wondered what they all had to do with my symptoms.

"You need to go the hospital within four hours," she said. "And if anything else happens, call an ambulance immediately."

That was a surprise.

"I need to go to the hospital," I told Peter.

Because I didn't know what time we'd get home, I made a couple of sandwiches. I didn't want my blood sugar levels to get too low if we were there a while.

When we got to the hospital, I wasn't isolated and given a Covid test as I expected. Peter waited in the reception area while I went into a different room. I waited a long time to see a doctor, overhearing other's troubles while I waited. I wasn't as bad as them. The lady behind the curtain next to me looked very unhappy. I wasn't unhappy.

A doctor came and asked more questions. I was given an MRI scan for the abdominal pains as well as one for the leg and neck pain. At 11:30pm I was still waiting for answers, so I took a quick selfie to let my Facebook friends know I was in hospital again.

I began to feel anxious for Peter who was still waiting in reception. I needed to tell him what was happening. But what was happening?

The doctor came back some time later and said they'd be keeping me in hospital. There were more tests to be done the following day.

"My husband is in reception," I said. "He's been waiting there about four hours. Can someone please tell him?" I was anxious about him not knowing what was happening and having to wait so long.

The doctor left the room quickly to speak to him.

I was given some strong medication that made me feel human again and my temperature began to go down.

A lady came in. At the time, I wasn't sure if she was a doctor or a nurse.

"I'm telling you this, so you won't wonder why you are going into the ward we are putting you in," she said.

She had my full attention. I *was* wondering, wondering what was coming next. She didn't immediately tell me the name of the ward.

"You will be seeing a doctor tomorrow," She continued. "He's a haematologist."

That didn't mean anything to me.

"We've looked at the scans."

She paused. It seemed to me she was thinking about her next words.

"A doctor in Canada has been consulted. She said it looks like cancer to her."

"Oh no!" I said.

"I'll give you something to help you sleep as you'll be upset," she said.

"No. I won't be. I already died once and Jesus put me back into my body, so I won't be upset. I've seen Jesus and love just pours out of Him."

The doctor looked surprised then smiled. "Did you?"

It had happened at a church meeting in Ashmore in 2018. The guest speaker had asked everyone to pair up and pray for each other. The lady who prayed for me, put her hands on my head and immediately I'd seen Jesus in the Spiritual realm. He was touching my brain and love was pouring out of Him. I'd never seen so much love emanating from anyone like this before. I could feel it going down into my brain. I could also feel the love He has for all the works of His hands. My soul began to weep deeply. If I'd been in the Spirit realm a moment longer my body would also have been on the ground weeping. At the time I thought Jesus must've been healing my brain, but He didn't. He had just loved it.

The doctor spoke in a very affirming manner. I was thirsty so asked if I could get a cup of water. She nodded.

As I walked across the room for a cup of water, the lady in the cubicle beside mine smiled a big smile at me. I nodded back to her. I thought maybe my testimony about Jesus had cheered her up. I hoped it had. It *had* taken the edge off the possibility of having cancer.

About 12am, I was taken to the oncology ward and sent a quick message to two of our daughters. "May have cancer." I thought I'd video message Roseanne, our youngest in the morning.

The following day, I woke with another fever. I didn't feel well.

The haematologist, whom I will call Dr Abba (meaning father) came to see me. Although younger than me, he had a calm, fatherly manner and I trusted him. He said I would get more fevers. I didn't want that and decided I'd ask people to pray so I wouldn't get more fevers.

"The scans showed enlarged lymph nodes," he said. "The leg and abdominal pain you are experiencing could be from that."

The blood tests showed a lot of inflammation, so that hadn't changed.

When the doctor left, I spoke to Peter on video messenger. Apparently, our eldest daughter, Natalie, had already read my message and spoken to him. She was very upset. Peter was upset too. He was also upset that I'd sent our girls such a short message. My news should've been shared face to face.

"I had a fever." I told him. "I didn't think about how upset everyone would be at such cryptic news. I just thought I needed to tell them I was in hospital and why."

"You might not have cancer," Peter said.

Natalie phoned. She still sounded very upset and repeated what Peter had said.

"You may not have cancer."

I told her a doctor in Canada had been consulted, and she had said it looked like cancer to her.

I video messaged our daughter, Aimee. She was upset too of course. I'd sent a less cryptic text message to our youngest daughter, Rosie. I hadn't mentioning cancer, just the enlarged lymph nodes and the need for a biopsy. I video messaged her the following day.

I messaged our church leader Bruce, to let him know what was going on and asked for prayer. I didn't want any more fevers.

Bent Over (c.2019)

I felt miserable. I told the Lord if I did have cancer and chemo, I couldn't see how that would bless others. I

30

imagined I'd be hanging out with the toilet in utter misery, wishing I could skip that part and just go to heaven. Others were so much better than I was with pain. I repeated myself. I didn't see how my moaning over a toilet bowl would glorify Him.

"I just don't cope well with nausea," I told Him as images of past episodes of vomiting came into my mind. Really, I was afraid of nausea and just wanted Him to rescue me from it all. I didn't want to go through all that.

"*Let me lead you through the chemo*," Jesus replied. His voice was so tender. It drew me close. Then I realised it really was cancer.

"Oh no! Not cancer."

I thought about how Jesus gave up so much for me. He gave up His life in heaven to come to earth. His gave up His life on earth and endured the cross for my joy. So, I reminded myself my life was His.

"I am yours," I said. I pictured myself taking his hand. I would let Him lead me even down this difficult path.

His word gave me the ability to trust which I thought I'd been lacking. I could trust His word even though He wasn't going to rescue me from having to have chemotherapy. I knew I had to go through it. He would lead me through it.

"*You are in my hand.*" That was what he'd said in July and now I knew why. He'd been preparing me.

That night, Saturday 28th August, I dreamt an evil lightning being was hurling electrical bolts at me, so I had to run into the nearest building to be safe. It was a big concrete building. Inside I saw a doctor, and had just missed seeing another one, so it was obviously a hospital. Did I need to be in hospital for a while to be safe? If so, I was in the right place.

I felt really well the following morning.

"You didn't get a fever," Doctor Abba said when he came in.

"No." I said. "I asked my church to pray for me."

He said he should repeat the blood tests to see what effect it had on my inflammation.

As he turned to leave, I saw an angel. The angel was wearing a white coat. It looked like a lab or a doctor's coat, although I couldn't remember seeing any doctors in this hospital wearing them. Doctor Abba didn't.

A wall of pastel-coloured boxes appeared near his hand. It suggested to me that the angel had a lot of resources available to him. I caught a glimpse of what looked like a very large syringe in his hand. It looked more like the kind you would use on an animal. He moved close to me and disappeared. I suddenly felt a kind of oneness with the angel. It was a moment of joyful surprise. Then the angel reappeared and walked very quickly out the door behind Doctor Abba. As he left, I felt something collapse where the large groin lumps were. Later I learnt this was where the inguinal lymph nodes were.

I touched the groin. I could feel the roundness of one of the nodes. The lumps were definitely smaller. The pain down my legs had gone too and never returned.

Later, during the day I had a conversation with one of the staff who came in. I can't remember if she was a nurse or a phlebotomist. I think she asked if I had any children. I told her I had three on earth and seven in heaven. I told her I'd had multiple miscarriages. In 1996 I'd seen a group of the ones I'd miscarried dancing in heaven. One of them had told me they were happy waiting for me there.

The nurse asked me how one got to see spiritual things. I told her what Jesus had said. One needed to be born again to see the kingdom of God.[5] Later I wished I'd told her how to be born again as she didn't ask. Seeing spiritual things is a gift available to every believer according to John who wrote that everyone believing that Jesus is the Christ and son of God has been born again.[6]

By late afternoon I was feeling very unwell again. I thought prayer was like daily bread. I needed it from the body of Christ every day. Today I needed more than one serving.

A CT Pet scan had been ordered for Wednesday 1st September, so I was put on a limited diet. No sauce, no sugar. I was already gluten free, diabetic and lactose free so no lots of things. What could I eat? They brought me vegetables with gluten free soy sauce. I took a mouthful, and it tasted so good. Then I remembered. I wasn't supposed to be having sauces. Agh! When I asked about it, I was told the kitchen staff said it was gluten free! Well, at least they got that right! They can't have received my new diet.

One of the servers came to my rescue. He took away the sauce covered meal and made me some food I could eat. I know all people are *"wonderfully made,"* but some are like wonders to us.[7] This man was one of those. His name was Mark. I wanted to remember it.

Later that morning I read an encouraging word by Sylvia Neusch.[8]

"Do the hard thing," she'd heard the Lord say.

That resonated with me. Chemo was a hard thing.

"Will you not trust in Me?"

---

[5] John 3:3

[6] 1John5:1 & 5

[7] Psalm 139:14

[8] (Neusch, 2021)

My trust wasn't as wobbly now that I had Jesus' word to cling to. He was going to lead me through this.

Sylvia had also written, *"You will emerge stronger and with EMPOWERED WINGS that lift and carry you through the difficulty ..."*[9]

That sounded so good. Empowered wings for someone whose online nickname had been Winging. That was me. I was soaring on eagle wings.[10]

Wings to soar (2021)

---

[9] (Neusch, 2021)
[10] Isaiah 40:31

Chapter 4 ∼ The Diagnosis

Push Off (2020)

On Tuesday the 31st, when Doctor Abba came in on his regular morning round, he said I may not have had bursitis. He was hoping to have some answers after the CT Pet scan in the afternoon and if it could be treated in hospital, he'd start treatment then. He was going to be away for a week so another haematologist would see me while he was away. I'll call him Doctor Paul. He would get things started.

In the afternoon, I was wheeled in my bed to another room for a guided biopsy. The biopsy was taken from the groin area next to where I'd felt the lumps collapse.

The following afternoon, Peter took me to South Coast Radiology for the Pet scan. I'd had Pet scans before, but this time the noise made me want to laugh. I tried not to, but some chuckles did escape.

That evening, back in the oncology ward, a message began blaring out over the loudspeaker. "The fire alarm system has operated. Stand by for further instruction."

When it finally stopped, I overheard the nurses saying there'd been a fire. At first, they thought it was outside, then someone said it was upstairs. It reminded me of the evil lightning in the dream I'd had.

On Thursday morning, the 2nd of September I heard God say to me very tenderly, *"My girl."*

I nearly cried. He is so affirmative.

I listened to Hillsong United music on Spotify and the song, *"Oceans (where my feet may fail,"* came on.[11]

Spirit lead me where my trust is without borders …
Take me deeper than my feet could ever wander …

The words reminded me of a vision I'd had in church in 2020. I'd made a sketch of it.[12] In the vision I saw myself standing on a wharf. Then I was in the water and heard a voice say, "Push off. Push off." I looked around for a boat but saw none. God was calling me out into the deep waters. At the time I wasn't sure how I was meant to put this into practice, but now I knew. The words of the song brought revelation. Now I was there in those deep waters, there where my feet would not have led me. I wanted my trust to be without borders. I yielded myself into God's hands again.

I played the song repeatedly, singing softly so as not to annoy anyone in the corridor or in the room next door.

Later I asked a nurse if it was okay to sing.

---

[11] (Crocker et al., 2013)
[12] Page 35

"Yes, sing," she said.

She told me no one could hear me outside my room, so that freed me up a bit. I got out of bed and danced gently around my room.

Dancer (1969)

A definite diagnosis of cancer still hadn't been given. According to the CT report, what they saw could be *"infective aetiologies including granulomatous disease/mycobacterial infection,"* although they did consider it less likely than Lymphoma.

Being in hospital had a strange effect on me. A single word would trigger memories of trauma and hospital. It was as if my brain was trying to classify and slot this new experience somewhere akin to an old one. It reminded me a bit of post-traumatic stress disorder.

On Friday the 3rd September two friends, Kerry and Graeme came to visit me in hospital. It was so lovely to see them. They brought me some gluten free food which was very thoughtful of them. While they were there, Doctor Abba also came in. He placed a copy of the scan report face down on my table. My friends made moves to go, but he said they could stay. They listened with me as he told us the results of the scan.

"You have a very aggressive form of Lymphoma," he said. A biopsy would give a more definitive diagnosis. "You have some enlarged lymph nodes. They are normally the size of a pea. That may be what's causing your leg pain." He spent some time speaking to us.

I felt quite calm. I had God's promise to lead me. Much later Kerry told me she'd been amazed at how calm I was, while she'd been shocked and tried not to show it.

After they left, I read the report the doctor had left for me. It said, what was seen was most suggestive of lymphoma and particularly Non-Hodgkins Lymphoma. The scans showed lymph node enlargement and soft tissue stranding surrounding some of the enlarged lymph nodes possibly reflecting *"extracapsular extension of tumour."* There was some compression of the left renal vein and much of the colon had collapsed as well.

The following day Doctor Paul filled in for Dr Abba. He was a younger man and like most who came into the room, he wore a mask, so I would not have recognised him in the street. A nurse came in with him. I told them Jesus had said, *"Let me lead you through the chemo."*

"So, I guess I'll have to go through the chemo," I said. I'd forgotten about the angelic visitor the day before. "I won't be miraculously healed this time."

The assisting nurse nodded. The doctor looked thoughtful.

In the afternoon, our friends, John and Maureen came to visit. They brought a beautiful flower arrangement, which gave me something lovely to look at. John told me his doctor had suspected he had cancer, and he had prayed in earnest for healing and was healed.

"Well, that's a much better testimony than me blubbing over the toilet," I said, thinking that was what I was about to go through. I had no idea what chemotherapy was like. However, Jesus' offer to guide me was so gentle, I wanted to trust Him in this. I repeated the words Jesus had said and turned my focus from the toilet back to Him. As I did, my trust became even less wobbly. He would lead me and surely, He would help me.

I had been eating a lot more than normal, so I found it hard to believe I'd lost two kilos since I came into hospital. I hadn't done any exercise to use the calories up either. All I managed to do was 1000 steps around my room most days since the fevers stopped. Weight loss was always good news from my perspective.

Doctor Paul came on the Friday and didn't want to sit facing me, but I told him I couldn't see him, so he moved. There were tears in his eyes as he gave me the bad news.

He said I had Diffuse large B-cell lymphoma with very aggressive and very large lymph nodes in the pelvis, abdomen, thoracic and thorax areas. Later I saw the pet scan results and the largest lymph node in the aortocaval position measured 55mm x 37mm x 121mm.[13]

Doctor Paul was worried about how I felt about losing my hair. I laughed. I told him I was more concerned about losing my brain cells. He said I would have five to six months of chemo but would need to have an echocardiogram first to see if my heart could cope with it.

I was encouraged by his compassion and didn't want him to feel bad about it. So, before he left, I said, "If anything

---

[13] The Pet scan results can be seen on page 157.

happens, and I'm not expecting it to, don't worry. I am looking forward to heaven."

I was. I had been longing for another visit there, but if it was a forever stay, that was okay too. It wouldn't be okay for all my friends and family, though, as they loved me so much. Our three girls had just sent a large bouquet of roses, and it touched me deeply. I felt very loved by everyone and less like leaving permanently.

In hospital holding roses from our children

I let my Facebook friends know I was holding Jesus' hand. He had always been faithful. I asked them to keep praying for me because it made a difference to how well I overcame. I could feel it when they prayed. Among other things, peace and light would envelope me.

I had the recommended echocardiogram to make sure my heart would cope, and the results were okay.

I saw one of Doctor Abba's colleagues on Saturday. I will call her Doctor Sue. She said there was widespread activity in the bone marrow where the lymphoma begins. It was stage four lymphoma, but it wasn't like other cancers. It was highly treatable.

On Monday, she came in with a nurse and gave me midazolam for the bone marrow biopsy on the hip. Under this anaesthetic apparently, I told her I was still awake, and it was stinging.

"No. You're not," Doctor Sue said.

I was glad she gave me a memory blocking injection, so I didn't remember the conversation or the pain, only a small memory of it stinging in the beginning.

When the results arrived back, Doctor Sue let me know they were fine. Later I read the bone marrow chromosome report dated the 6th September and it did indeed say, *"no abnormalities were detected."* The cancer hadn't spread to my bones. That was a relief.

Some weeks later when Doctor Sue filled in for Doctor Abba again, I asked her if I'd said anything rude while under the anaesthetic. She laughed and assured me I hadn't. That was also a relief!

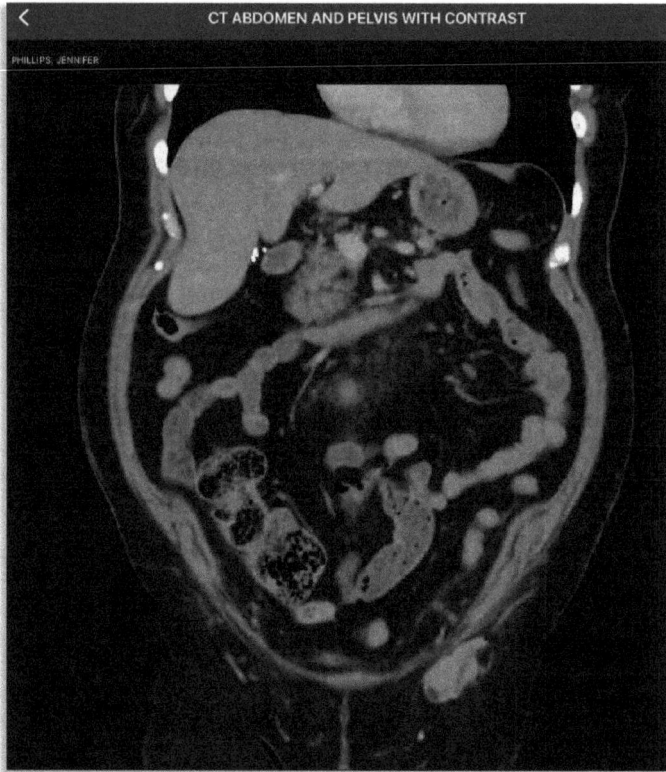

Scan showing enlarged lymph nodes (27 August 2021)

Chapter 5 ❦ The First Cycle 6/9/21

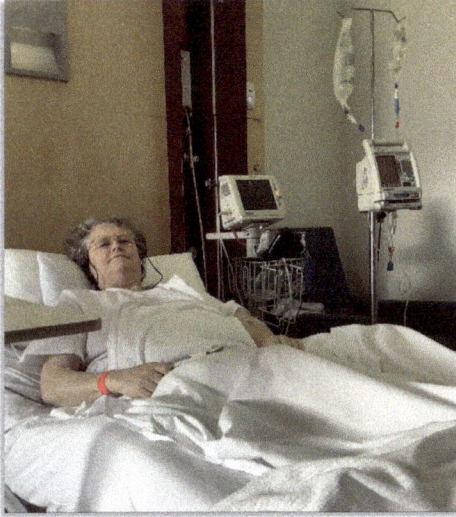

First lot of chemotherapy administered via a drip

I took my black cardigan off and placed it on the grey padded armchair. A framed picture was hanging on the hospital wall above it. Somehow it seemed significant, so I stood for a while looking at it. There were plants hanging down over river water and more were tangled on a sandy bank. They looked almost dead. I turned to look at the other picture in the room. It was a close-up view of plants on possibly the same sandy bank. The plants nearly merged into the background. They contrasted sharply with the bright blue of the monitor on the mobile IV drip stand that had been wheeled in for the chemo drip.

Two rubbish bins had also been brought into the room. They were bright as well. One was purple and the other had a red lid. A nurse had spent some time educating me about what was going to happen, and what I should and shouldn't do. Chemotherapy I was told was a strong, cytotoxic (toxic to cells) medicine, so it was important that any body fluids on paper towels etc went into the cytotoxic waste bins, so others would not be harmed.

Except for four Prednisolone tablets, the chemotherapy was administered through a drip into a vein. The first lot was Rituximab, which started at 11.24am. It's a targeted immunotherapy that deals with the B cells. They ran it through slowly to make sure I didn't have any allergic reactions. It took six hours. After that, I had three others, which made up the RCHOP combination. They finished at around 7.30pm, a total of about eight hours.

I wasn't given the normal premedication (antihistamine) because I have bad reactions to some, but thankfully I had no adverse reactions to the chemotherapy on day one of the cycle. I was given anti-nausea medication though, which I was so pleased about. However, I still had a fear of nausea … and that was day one of the first cycle.

That night, I didn't sleep much. Apparently, that's one of the side effects of Prednisolone.

Towards the morning of day two, my neck glands suddenly popped out. They were painful and made it hard to swallow. As they pressed in on my throat, I panicked. For a moment, I couldn't breathe. I leapt out of bed and started walking around the room praying silently. I thought walking would stop the glands from pressing down on my throat so much. It did.

I sent an urgent message to Len, our church prayer leader. The response was immediate. He sent the praying hands icon back. I was surprized he was awake at that time. I didn't know some of the church met at 5:30am to pray every day. The moment I received the reply the glands began to go down a bit. I then sent out a request for prayer to my Facebook friends.

When Doctor Paul arrived for the regular hospital visit, he checked my glands and said it was normal for steroid treatment. He said my glands were still a fair size. I was glad they had improved enough so I could swallow without pain.

Doctor Paul said I was full of disease, that's why he had started the treatment so quickly.

On day two of each cycle, I would be given an injection to stimulate the bone marrow to produce more white cells. I'd been told it made people feel like they had the flu.

However, Doctor Paul said, "Not everyone feels like they have the flu after the second day injection."

I immediately prayed that I would be one of those who didn't have flu-like symptoms.

In the evening, I began feeling nauseous, so I nibbled on a biscuit. I slept for an hour and then nibbled on the biscuit again. I fell asleep but woke an hour later feeling bilious. I began moaning. I didn't want to be on this path. The anti-nausea medication was supposed to last three to five days. The doctors had tricked me! I'd been told most people find the first week good and the second week "crap." On the third week of the cycle, they start to come right again. If this was the good week …

An image flashed across my vision. It was a group of army men on a military exercise. They were so completely in step with each other, they looked as though they were glued together.

I needed to go to war! So, I told the Lord I needed to hear His voice if I was going to be able to follow His lead.

"You'll get through this," He said.

I began using some of David's cries to the Lord from the psalms I remembered.

Hear my cry God, prick up you ears.
From the ends of the earth I will call
when my heart is overwhelmed.
Lead me to the cliff that is higher than I.
... Let me dwell in your tent forever...[14]

I slept again and when I woke, I called the nurse. She said I could have a nausea tablet. Oh? I didn't know that! I took it and had a good three-hour sleep. When I woke, I felt good again. I was so thankful.

I thought about the injection I'd be given in the evening. The one that could give flu-like symptoms. Oh joy! Another nighttime battle!

I felt so weak but reminded myself that God was strong and faithful.

The Lord answered my prayer. I *was* one of those who didn't get flu-like symptoms. Either that or I slept through them. Instead of being awake from the steroids, I had the best sleep I'd had for a long time. I had 5 hours with a break when I was semi woken for meds. That seemed like a miracle because I'd been told I should have been awake because of the steroids. I had been awake the first night.

The following morning, I had the most amazing visions. It reminded me of Terragen, a scenery generating computer program I used to use, where one can move around in the environment, zoom in and out, and see things from whatever angle is desired.

In different visions, I was led beside restful waters. Some were wide rivers with dark brown hills on either side. Some were narrow rivers and streams. Some of the streams

---

[14] Psalm 61

had rushes growing along the bank and in the waters. Some had stones and mud. Sometimes the sun shone in, and in some areas, there was sunset light. A few places had only mud with patches of water.

My first memoir

Along one was a tall mud bank. The Holy Spirit and I zoomed slowly in for a closer look. It was better than TV and so restful, yet amazing. All I could think of was, restful waters.

Later that day, I received a basket of flowers with a teddy bear from my mother. My sister Kath had helped her organize it. When I held the bear, I was surprised by a wave of comfort. It really was a comfort bear! I thought only children would feel that way, but I did.

A nurse came into the room. She told me she was reading my memoir, "Let me travel with you." She said one of the nurses had left it for everyone to read. I was glad my life was being shared. I'd prayed many times that it would be a blessing to others.

In the evening, the Lord did the morning miracle again. He gave me visions of still waters, only this time they were all heart shaped. It was an amazing wonder.

I read Psalm 23 and, *"He will make me lie upon lush pastures and he will lead me by restful waters,"* stood out. The word, make stood out and I smiled. Sometimes He Makes! Today He had made me lie down. The pasture was lush and the waters restful.

However, in the night, I sent Len another urgent prayer request. I'd been accidentally given gluten in an evening meal and developed bleeding sores in my nose and my checks were still flushed from the chemotherapy. He immediately messaged back saying he'd

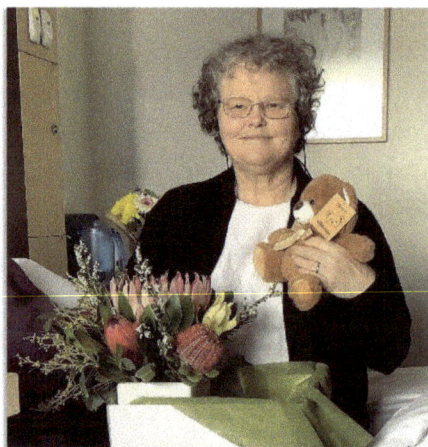

My mother's gift of comfort

prayed, and the flush left, the bleeding stopped, and the swollen glands reduced further.

The following day Jenny, one of the ladies who worked in the office at Genesis Church at that time, came to visit me in hospital. My friend Nicola also worked in the office and was glad for the opportunity to come too. They brought a basket of yellow flowers—a gift from the church. It was as though they'd brought a basket of sunshine. They also prayed for me and some of the stinging cramping stomach pains I had eased. They let me know others were praying for me too. I was so thankful.

While praying, Nicola had a vision. She saw our heavenly Father holding my hand and leading me through a field of flowers. She didn't know I'd held out my hand and imagined I was putting it in God's hand. The vision was so encouraging. God *was* holding my hand. The vision also reminded me of what the Lord had said a few days earlier. He *was* leading me.

About twenty-two years before, a friend had also had a vision of me in a field of flowers. That was interesting.

The following day, the 10th September I woke with deep peace in my mind.

"My soul is restored," I told a nurse.

"What do you call an unbeliever? she said.

"I don't know," I said. "An unbeliever?"

Flowers from Genesis Church

"Nurse X is an unbeliever," she said.

"No, I'm not," Nurse X said. "I was brought up with Christian values."

The other nurse pointed to me, "She's seen Jesus."

Nurse X said, "I know. She told me."

I *have* seen Jesus and love pours out of Him. I gave nurse X the last copy of my memoir.

A friend, Tracy, came to visit. She'd had cancer the previous year and gave me a pile of chemo hats.[15] My hair was expected to fall out in a week or two, so they would be useful. Our daughter Natalie also bought me a chemo hat. It arrived the same day. I felt blessed. Somehow these gifts brought peace with them.

The following day, being the weekend, a female doctor came instead of Doctor Paul. I still had abdominal pains. The sharp jabbing pain in the appendix area had returned as well. I felt so thankful to the doctor when she touched the sore spot, and I leapt with pain. It was identified and seen

---

[15] Hats made with the needs of cancer patients in mind.

at last. She said I wouldn't be able to have the appendix out, so she hoped it wasn't that. She thought the pain could be diverticulitis. Whatever it was, I had to go onto a free fluid diet. Yuk.

Nicola, my friend from church phoned, and we prayed in tongues together.[16] It was so good to be able to pray in our special languages because I would not have been able to say everything I was feeling. In tongues, I was able to completely pour my heart out to God. Our time together was so lovely. As we prayed, the Holy Spirit said I would go out with joy. I believed it. I would go out at some time with joy. The Lord would deliver me from all my troubles just as He had for David.[17]

Because my diet had been changed to the free fluids one, somehow, I didn't get any lunch. I waited for it and fretted. I was diabetic and couldn't bear the feeling of low blood sugars. It made me feel like I would die if I didn't eat something. I thought, maybe the Lord was helping me to overcome my fear of not eating regularly. I reminded him I could depend on Him to lead me through this too. I would trust Him for the food I needed.

Lunch still didn't arrive. I asked the staff about it. I became hungry and fretted again, then I trusted the Lord again. I did get through it but was so glad when the evening meal arrived.

Being the weekend, another different doctor visited me.

"You'll get through this," she said.

I told her that's what Jesus had said to me too, so I knew I would. She had such a lovely smile I could see it in her eyes. The mask didn't mask it.

_____

[16] Speaking in tongues is a Holy Spirit empowerment we both had.
[17] Psalm 54:7

50

On Monday the 13th September, Doctor Abba was back. He ordered some blood tests.

I was glad my hospital room was like a hotel. My bed was made for me every day and it was so comfortable. I thought it must be one of the best I've slept in. Maybe it was the pain relief I'd been given! My food was brought to me too. All I needed to do was press a buzzer and sooner or later a nurse would come to "wait upon me."

I even had a chemo navigator. I asked her what it meant to "feel crap"—the normal feeling for the second week of the chemo cycle. I wanted to know in case I thought some symptoms were just part of feeling crap and I ignored them. "It's feeling tired," she said.

I laughed. Was that all? I'd been feeling like that a lot since the first Covid jab. I could cope with that. All I needed to do was take a few naps.

Things were looking better and better. No crap week coming up after all. Maybe I'd glide like a deer in the forest even during chemo.

One of the tablets I was on apparently made me talkative. Whether it was that or not, when a cleaner came in, I chatted with her as she cleaned.

I discovered her brother had recently died, so I told her about how I had died and how Jesus had resurrected me. She'd never heard of anyone coming back alive after dying, so I also told her of a time I went to one room in heaven while under anaesthesia. The room in heaven had been filled with light. I'd seen two men in white robes either side of me. They were instructing me, and another man in white had been standing by a white board (before such things as white boards had been invented). At the time, I didn't want to go back to earth but I wasn't given a choice. I started going back through a long dark tunnel into the hospital room. The closer I got to my body the more pain I felt. From the top of the hospital room, I had seen the anaesthetist by the wall looking at a monitor.

He had said, "She's starting to be distressed."

I was. I felt so distressed.

Then the surgeon said, "Just a bit more, I'm at the …"

I didn't recognise the part of the body he was at. The next thing I remembered was waking up crying. A nurse was beside me. She said I'd been crying for a long time. I think she said an hour or so.

Because of this traumatic experience, now whenever I have surgery, I'm given memory-blocking medicine, so I won't remember anything and be traumatised by the pain. Thankfully I'm not allergic to it …

I told the cleaner our bodies were mortal, but we weren't. The cleaner was so amazed, and I enjoyed sharing, only it must have put my blood pressure up because afterwards it was high again!

The pain in the appendix area that made me leap when the Doctor had touched it disappeared. I was amazed at how quickly it went. I still had some other twinging pains, but they weren't as angry as before.

Doctor Abba said my kind of lymphoma comes up quickly but can go down just as quickly with the chemo.

"That's the aim," he said. He was expecting a complete healing.

I was cheerful and sometimes felt so well, I didn't feel like I had anything wrong … and this was the second week of the first cycle! The one when I was supposed to feel crap. Not so far! I was just tired with a few stomach pains.

Later that day some nurses wearing protective clothing arrived. They put a sign on my door letting the other nurses know they had to wear protective clothing when they come in my room. They told me it was to protect me, not them from me.

I was startled. Like a deer, my body was instantly on high alert. I'd only just yielded my time in hospital into Jesus' hands. I had been feeling so well. I thought I'd be going home the following day. Was I now going to be in for a long time?

My blood test results had come back and showed my immunity had dropped even further. My neutrophils should have been above 1, as the average for chemo patients was 1.5. Mine were 0.5.

A few days before I had declared the Lord my immunity, protector and keeper. I'd asked Him to send His angels to surround me. He *had* sent angels, because when Nicola and I were praying together, she saw them in a vision. She didn't know what I'd prayed. That night, I prayed again for God's protection and sent out prayer requests.

When I woke the following day the insides of my lips were swollen. It felt like the skin had rubbed off. I had oral thrush. I didn't feel as well.

Doctor Paul arrived. He said I would be safer at home than in hospital. He said the stomach pain I'd had was probably constipation. I told him I know what that pain is like. It wasn't that. He said the gripes in the bowel were what some got with chemo. He sighed as he left the room.

I began to fret. I didn't think I would cope at home. What if I got a tick bite? Even though I'd seen the chemo educator, I'd forgotten a lot of what she'd said. I didn't really understand about low neutrophils. Did they stay low the whole time? I was very upset. I overreacted and voiced my worry. "I don't know anything!"

Suddenly a few nurses appeared. One gave me a booklet with information about neutropenia. I read it and calmed down. I'd misunderstood some of what the educator had said even though she'd given me the same booklet to read. It didn't seem like I'd read it.

A nurse came in and said they would remove the flowers. I didn't know that even pollen could be dangerous for me. She put the flowers outside the room and a stop sign on my door. It had instructions for all visitors. Any who entered had to put on a gown, gloves and mask and keep the door closed at all times, and everyone had to see the nurse in charge prior to entering.

I slipped into fretting again, then remembered the Lord's promise to lead me. It was a bit late, but I chose to stop fretting, as I knew it led to evil doing, and I had overreacted. I felt so bad about overreacting.

Twice that night the Lord said, *"I am with you in this."* I needed this repetition.

The following day someone sent me a Bible verse. It confirmed what I'd heard the Lord say.

The Lord Himself goes before you and will be with you. He will never leave you nor forsake you. Do not be afraid; Do not be discouraged.[18]

This message wasn't the only thing that encouraged me. I was a card-making demonstrator and regularly went to the Lorikeet demonstrator group. Many of the ladies had sent cards and the leader Anna, along with Michelle, Donna and Mary-Anne had put together a care pack of things I might need in hospital. I did need them. Among the items were warm socks and lip-balm. Our daughters also sent care packs, and their thoughtfulness really helped me.

---

[18] Deuteronomy 31:8, New International Version

The next morning, Doctor Abba answered the questions I had fretted about the day before. He arranged for another blood test. I felt such relief. He said my last blood test showed I was a bit anaemic, but some of the inflammation had come down. He said not to make any big decisions during the chemo treatment.

That reminded me of what the Lord had said just before I went into hospital. A real estate agent had suggested we put our property on the market, but the Lord had said to wait. God had known what was coming up and now wasn't the time for a big decision like moving, that I did know.

Doctor Abba also spoke about the unknown and death. "You need to prepare for death," he said.

I grinned. I assured him death wasn't a problem as I'd died once before.

"Yes, you did," he said.

I'd given him my memoir to read. He *had* read it. I should have added, it's the idea of long bouts of nausea and pain that trips me up.

Later, I reminded myself not to be afraid of nausea and pain.

In the afternoon, the nurses came and changed the sign again. I was surprized the blood tests had come back so quickly. My neutrophil levels had come up. They were no longer below the normal range for people on chemo. They were up towards the top of normal range for everyone. They were 7.2. The average range was 2-7.5. With chemo they expected them to rise slowly. Mine had risen quickly. I was amazed. I let those I'd asked to pray know their prayers for my neutrophils had been answered.

On the 16th September when Doctor Abba came, I told him I wasn't afraid of death. I was afraid of nausea and some kinds of pain made me panic.

"The dying process," he said.

"Yes," I replied. The dying process was what it was called. Now I had the language to communicate what I meant.

He began to allay my fears. He said I was

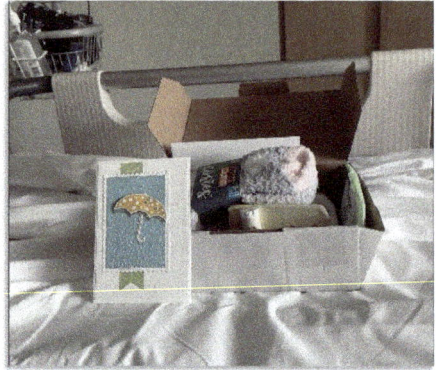
A care box from Lorikeet Stampers group

on tablets to help prevent various infections and my body was beginning to be able to fight infections again. My next lot of chemo would be Monday week if my blood tests were okay. Then I'd go through it again, only I'd be an outpatient and know what to expect. All going well I would have a total of six lots of chemo.

I remembered Doctor Abba telling me my kind of cancer comes up very quickly but can also go down very quickly too. I was hopeful. The leg pains hadn't returned. The stinging in my tongue had gone and the difficulty swallowing hadn't become worse, so I felt confident I'd cope at home.

Chapter 6 ⊰ Back Home

Tall Trees (2013)

The view from our main bedroom at home was lovely. It was filled with tall gum trees that had inspired me to do a few quick watercolour paintings. On the right, I'd planted a Tibouchina. When in flower, it splashed the view with purple. From time to time, when I looked out the sliding door, the Holy Spirit had let me know it would be a great place to be when recovering from a sickness. Sometimes it had seemed like that was going to happen. My bedroom would be a sickroom. I didn't like that thought so didn't entertain it, nor had I ever asked God about it.

Now as I looked, I saw tall weeds on the bank. However, the overgrown garden didn't spoil the view for me. I looked above them.

I was struck by how quiet and peaceful it was at home. It was Saturday and felt like a weekend after work. I found myself relaxing and was surprised. I'd been very atmospherically and environmentally sensitive recently. The stimulation of people and noise in hospital over the last few days had disturbed me without my normal awareness. Doctor Paul was right. He'd said it was safer for me to be at home at this time. He was probably thinking of my low neutrophils, but I was thinking of my state of mind.

I discovered my card-making friends had sent lovely cards. It was very encouraging. My church family at Genesis and other churches were so supportive too, not just in prayer and chatting online, giving flowers and cards, but in some of the practical things. Kerry made a gluten and sugar free cake, and meals for me. Maureen had brought gluten free brownies to the hospital with the flowers. Alberto and another friend brought meals for Peter, and Marg, who'd also had cancer, phoned me in hospital and encouraged me with a long chat. She became a supportive online friend during the chemo, as did others from church.

The first morning back home, I woke an hour later than I had done in hospital and felt quite lightheaded. It was only 5.30am. Alberto had promised to leave a meal for Peter by the front door on his way out, which was about then, so I sat with all my discharge tablets in front of me. It felt like too big a job to sort out what I was supposed to take.

While I was thinking this, Alberto arrived and asked if I wanted help sorting them. I told him I thought I would manage. He asked to use the bathroom. I told him I hadn't cleaned it, and he said he would come back and do some cleaning for me. He stayed and chatted, and I was greatly encouraged.

After he left, I thought I would be able to mop some floors, but after cleaning one toilet and the kitchen benchtop, I had to spend the rest of the morning on my bed. I was exhausted and had strong right sided abdominal pain.

I enjoyed some time on my bed listening to a Bible reading and some Bethel church music. In the Bible reading I heard an unusual translation for Psalm 40. Either that or the Lord changed the words.

I heard, *"The thoughts of the Lord are more numerous than the hairs on your head."* I checked my hair to see if it was about to fall out as on the very day her hair fell out, Rosemary, a friend, just happened to read the Bible verse, *"Even the hairs on your head are numbered."*[19]

Alberto mopping our floors

"I'll let you keep your hair," a voice said in my mind.

I didn't want to believe it was the Lord. The truth was, I was looking forward to wearing all my new hats and not going to the hairdresser. I was looking forward to it growing back all the same length so it might be curly all over like my mother's. Maybe it would be white all over like hers too. I loved the look of her hair. I'd just had a long chat on the phone with her. I loved her so much. Her video messaging had been out of action all the time I was in hospital so I couldn't see or speak to her. At last, I'd been able to phone so she wouldn't be too worried about me.

That day, the 20th September, I was glad I still had all my hair for the Lord to count! I told the Lord I didn't mind

---

[19] English Standard Version

one way or the other, hair or no hair. Whatever glorified Him the most.

"That's my girl," I heard Him say.

His words were so tender and comforting. Smiling, I repeated them to myself. *"My girl."* I was His. It made me feel safe. So, would I get to wear my hats or give them away?

Later that day, Alberto came back and mopped our floors. I felt the wonder of his kindness.

I continued lying on my bed and twice the Holy Spirit said to get up. So, I went down to the pool and cleaned the filter box. It was full of leaves, which usually causes the cleaner to stop working. It hadn't! I saw a water-boatman in the water. I got the skimmer, and I tried to catch the water-boatman, but wasn't sure if I did.

I felt a bit unsteady on my feet and brushed up against a plant. It pricked me. What was it they said about being careful not to get any cuts? I made a mental note to be more careful there. I pulled a couple of weeds then remembered I was supposed to wear gloves and not touch any compost. I gave my hands a good wash afterwards.

It was no longer painful to swallow, but on showering, I had a few sharp pains below. I wondered if I should take two showers a day.

I hadn't woken drenched in sweat during the night — the first time maybe all year. I just had some light sweating. I was, however, still sweating during the day. I checked my sugars before lunch, and they were just under 10. Maybe my sugars were making me sweat. Whatever the reason, my sugar levels were still too high.

The following day when I went to brush my hair, I saw a lot of hairs in the brush. It was falling out right on schedule! I chuckled as I thought about what the Lord had said the day before. I would get to wear all the lovely hats

I'd been given after all. I'd get to skip the hairdresser and didn't need to wash my hair. I was surprised at how quickly it was coming out. It was falling all over the house, so I cut it shorter. I wondered how long it would take before it was all

Standing beside my unfinished artwork - Stepping Stones (2021)

gone. I didn't know it wouldn't *all* go. I would get to keep some as well, only it looked odd having tuffs of hair, so I ended up cutting it all off.

I was sent Isaiah 40:31 and translated it as, *"Those who gather to the Lord shall renew their strength."* So, as I had no energy the next day, I walked around in the evening singing and praying in tongues and felt strength come into me. I had enough strength to mop some of the floors in the house for the first time since coming out of hospital. However, I didn't have enough mental energy to add a few brush strokes to an artwork I was working on. It was based on a vison I'd had in church of stepping stones. I only had enough to stand in front of it and smile for a photo!

I needed to see my GP. She said she'd been really gutted when she heard about my diagnosis. I told her I was so glad she was my doctor. I told her I didn't mind if I lived or died because I've seen Jesus, but my family love me so much I want to be here for them.

The apostle Paul said, *"For to me, to live is Christ, and to die is gain. However, to live in the body will mean fruitful labour for me."*[20] I felt the same way. I had felt like this since I was a young Christian. However, even though Doctor Abba had initially said to prepare for death, he was expecting a full recovery, as Lymphoma when treated had a very high success rate. The Lord had said I would get through this, but I wasn't sure what the Lord had in mind after I got through it. Would I live long afterwards?

As I read the Bible, I could feel the heart of God, for His people in the words from Deuteronomy *"... let me dwell with you in this place."* All I knew of my future right then was that God's desire was to dwell with me, and it wasn't time to sell our house just yet. I didn't have a current word about living long on this earth, so I didn't put any hope in doing so.

It has never happened before, and just when I had to be very careful about not getting any cuts, Peter's toenail cut my foot in bed. Apparently with chemo, cuts don't go red and can be missed, but mine was a very bright red as though someone had painted it as a warning flag, so I saw it. One wouldn't think a toenail could make such a big cut. Why was it important not to get cuts? I couldn't remember. I asked my Facebook friends to pray for it.

Peter was ready to take me to pathology for another blood test. I told him to wait a bit as I wasn't quite ready to go. A moment later, the doorbell rang. I thought I recognised the lady behind her mask. I thought she was from church, so I asked her if she was well.

"Come in," I said.

It was just as well I'd told Peter to wait a bit otherwise we would have missed her. She said she was from Aged Care. I'd never met her before! I'd forgotten she was coming! I was glad she was who she said she was. Perhaps in the

---

[20] Philippians 1:21-22

future I would ask people to take off their mask so I could see who they were before inviting them in!

The lady asked many questions and when she asked about allergies, I shared my experience of dying, and Jesus' miracle of healing and resurrection. She asked what church I went to, and I was able to testify about how I ask them to pray, and how I'd been healed of the fevers, and how Alberto brought a meal and mopped my floor. She asked if I had any depression.

"No," I said. "I have the joy of the Lord, apart from one day in hospital when I fretted and overreacted, like I'd never done before." I told her I was looking forward to heaven, when the time came, but I also wanted to be here for my children. I told her how supportive they and friends had been. She smiled.

I'm eligible for some help, but the transport is a group one, and the people will all be going for medical appointments, so that wouldn't be good for me. I needed to avoid crowded places and stay away from people who were unwell.

When her visit ended, Peter took me for the blood test and afterwards Nicola phoned. We had a long prayer time together. Again, it was so wonderful. Church at home on the phone!

As we prayed, I had a vision of someone on a darkish path with the light in the distance. I heard the words, *"No path is too difficult for you,"* followed by the concept of, *because God is with me.* It was more than words and reminded me of Philippians 4:13, *"I have strength for all things in Christ who is the one who strengthens me."* I also saw a window and knew we must view things from God's perspective.

Nicola also had a vision. She saw a dove descending with peace. I began reminding myself that no path was *too difficult* for me and my trust in God deepened. I thought about how I now had tablets that worked for nausea and pain, unlike in the past when pain and nausea had traumatized me. As a result, fear of the dying process left.

Later, I heard a voice say, *"I want you back in hospital."* The words took me by surprise. I wasn't even praying at the time, so I had to ask, "Is that You Lord?"

I had an appointment with Doctor Abba. He told me there was hardly any inflammation left.

"Wow!" The wonder of it couldn't be held in.

He said he wanted me to stay in hospital for a few days after my next lot of chemo, to see what was happening with my temperatures. I felt my body relax when he said that. It confirmed what I'd heard. I was glad I'd be in hospital for the chemo because for the five days I was on Prednisolone my blood sugars were too high. My blood sugar monitor had stopped working too so I couldn't monitor them at home. Also, day patients only got a chair to sit in. I couldn't sit for 7-8 hours even in a reclining type of chair. I needed a bed!

On the 23rd September, my friend Paula asked if she could visit. Social contact was just what I needed so I said yes, even though I'd had a slight nosebleed that week. I had a headache, and my temperature was still raised, but I didn't have a fever. I was looking forward to seeing her again.

When I saw her, my joy filled up. She had not only thought of me, giving me flowers and a yummy gluten free tart, she'd also thought of Peter. She gave him one of his favourite lunches, a pie.

Praising God with a short arm dance

On the 28th September, I went in for the second lot of chemo. I was glad I had a single room and a bed to lie on as the chemo started at 3.30pm and didn't finish until 11pm.

I spent the rest of the evening chatting with two nurses. One said she wanted to stay and listen to me all night. She said she'd had so many signs pointing her to God and now me. I gave her my memoir, and she was pleased. I encouraged her to read the New Testament too. She said a friend had given her one in her own language. Our conversation cheered me up. The day before, the Lord had spoken to me about being the Father's witness and I had the opportunity I wouldn't have had if I'd been a day patient.

I woke the following morning with a pounding head, burning and flushed face, sharp pains in the lymph nodes, abdominal pains, diarrhoea and swollen glands in the neck. I felt like vomiting and had thrush, but miraculously after lunch, the chemotherapy reactions subsided. When Doctor Paul visited, he said I was opposite to others in my chemo reaction.

"That'd be me," I grinned. He wasn't the

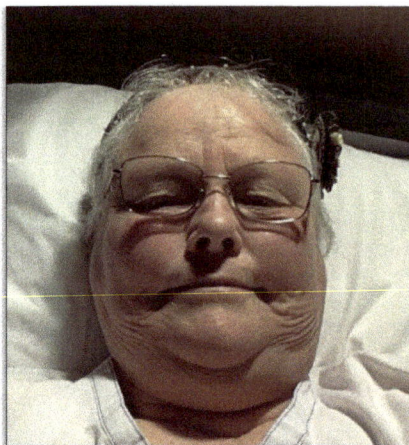

Swollen face after chemotherapy

first specialist to say I was different. Even my gallbladder was facing the opposite direction to other people. At the time, the surgeon who'd taken it out told me he'd had trouble finding it.

The following day Doctor Abba also said I was different from other people. The chemo makes most people constipated. I had diarrhoea. He asked if I thought I was well enough to go home today or tomorrow. I said I thought I'd be okay that day. I felt so much better. I wanted to do what he thought was appropriate.

A nurse came bustling into my room and put a new notice up.[21] No visitors were allowed in the hospital wards because of two Covid cases on the Gold Coast. Another notice was put on the inside of the door too. I was to follow the set rules listed there for 8 days following chemo, to protect others from my cytotoxicity.

I was worried about my high blood sugars (19.7). I didn't know it was only a problem if they stayed high

---

[21] Can be seen on page 158.

overnight. Because they were high, the nurse waited for Doctor Abba's consent. While I waited, I prayed anxiously about it, then surrendered the outcome into the Lord's hands. I had dinner in hospital and said to the Lord, "If they come down, I'll be happy to go home."

Amazingly they were one point lower an hour after my meal. Normally a meal puts them up, so I was confident I wouldn't have to come back in after getting home

Doctor Abba was happy for me to go home too, as my high blood sugars were caused by the Prednisolone and didn't stay high all night. Consequently, I got home late in the evening.

As I lay in bed night reading and praying, I knew what the Apostle Paul meant when he said, *"Therefore, I am well pleased in infirmities, in reproaches, in needs, in persecutions, in distresses, for Christ's sake. For when I am weak, then I am strong."*[22] I was pleased to be on the path because the Lord was leading me. I knew there were pleasures on the mountain and in the valleys, through the waters and fires. The valleys keep me leaning on Christ and I knew they were good for my character development. At that moment I felt in need of some character development. I wanted Christ to shine through me more. I wanted to fret less. I didn't know anxiety was a side effect of some of the chemo.

On Sunday, at the end of the first week of the second cycle of chemo, there was a storm. When it had passed, I ventured out into the garden to see what damage had been done. I could see a broken branch hanging precariously from one of the tall trees. I found some broken branches that needed chain sawing. They needed to be moved to clear the second driveway, but today I was only strong enough to

---

[22] 2 Corinthians 12:10

survey the area as I had an earache, headache and raised temperature.

It was the day when my neutrophils would be at their lowest. When I saw myself in a mirror, I looked like a ghost. During the previous cycle I was a bit anaemic at this point. Perhaps I was again.

I still had some hair. Maybe I would get to keep 10%. That made me chuckle. Keeping instead of giving a tithe. A tithe of my hair!

I slept most of the rest of the day.

I discovered something amazing. I no longer liked the taste of chocolate. I thought that could be a good thing … if it lasted. I didn't realise I'd lost my smell and most of my taste.

I began dreading going back for the third lot of Chemo. I'd been told many people found the last *two* cycles difficult. I'd only had two.

I Psalm 24 I read, *"Be of good courage and I will strengthen your heart."* Afterwards I checked my Facebook page and Gianni had written, "You have courage."

I felt a surge of joy. I was courageous? I felt sure this meant the Lord would strengthen my heart.

In different ways the Holy Spirit continued reminding me to be very courageous. So, whenever I thought about the upcoming chemo, I chose not to entertain the subjective thoughts about what I thought it would be like, based on what it had been like. I repeated God's words to me.

"We can do this," I told myself.

Every time I felt afraid of the chemo side effects, I engaged in spiritual warfare by reminding myself of what God had said. I said to Him, "No path is too difficult for me because You are with me."

"Chemo is progressive," I was told, so whenever that thought came into my mind, I replaced it with one of God's promises such as, *"I can do all things through Christ who strengthens me."* Travelling with Jesus is the best.

The following day I made some gluten free and dairy free bread. That and hanging out the washing was all I could manage, which was an improvement on the previous day. However, I still had throbbing in the ear, a headache, raised temperature and an ulcer on my tongue.

I was worse the following day. The throbbing was so loud it hurt my ear, and I had pain down my neck and behind the eye and I'd had bouts of sweating and nausea. I felt very unwell, so I rang the chemo navigator and ended up going back into hospital.

I waited on a bed in the emergency department. A blood test was done, and I continued waiting. After a few hours a nurse asked if I'd had an ECG. I hadn't, but one didn't eventuate. I was given a brain scan but thankfully nothing showed up on that.

I stayed in the hospital overnight and when Doctor Abba visited me, in the morning, on his daily rounds, he said he wanted me to have a quiet day in the hospital. My blood pressure had been high but was trending downwards, which was good. Using the so-so sign, he said there wasn't anything startling, that is unexpected in my blood test results. I'd read them yesterday, when they'd been left on my table. Quite a few readings were too high or too low as they usually were. He thought my heart rate had increased. I certainly had the symptoms of that. Now I had the language to describe what I was feeling.

The following day Nicola phoned and we were church together again. I had a vision of a palm branch and asked the Lord what He was saying. Later as I listened to some music, the song, *Raise A Hallelujah*, came on, so I did just that.[23] Then I knew what the Lord was saying in the vision. Praise! I turned my thoughts to Jesus and praised Him. He is my saviour and the victorious king. His kingdom is the blessed one. Hosanna! I got my dancing ribbons out

Me wearing the free Cancer Council wig

and let my arms dance a very short dance.

Peter suggested I get a wig. I agreed. I wasn't fond of the hundred-year-old look I had with my thinned out white hair. I thought I needed something a little more sophisticated than a chemo hat for some outings.

I'd heard from a friend that the Cancer Council had free wigs, so I made an appointment. On the 13th October, Peter took me to their rooms. I tried some dark-haired wigs, but they didn't suit me. I tried some blonde ones too. There was only one I liked, but I wasn't sure. The look was so different. When I asked Peter for his advice, he suggested I video message our daughter Aimee. I did. She liked the one I liked, so that was it. I loved my new look and smiled as I remembered how I'd wanted long straight blond hair as a teenager! Now however, I thought my age recommended a short cut!

---

[23] (Stevens et al., 2019)

Chapter 8 ⚜ The Third Cycle 18/10/21

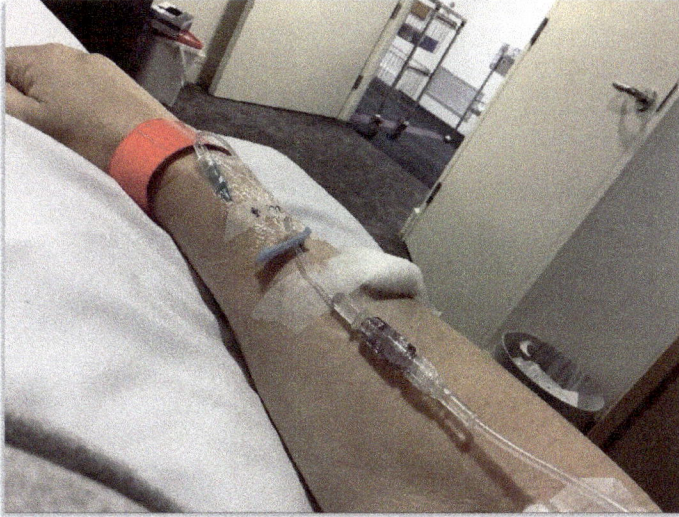

Receiving chemotherapy

A nurse had booked me in for the third chemo cycle. She said most of the others came in the day before, so she booked me in for the Sunday. So, on the 17th October, I arrived for my third lot.

The room was down the other end of the ward this time. It was quieter and had a lovely view. I watched people playing cricket through the gum trees and relaxed for a while.

The beds were normally comfortable, but it wasn't this time. My neck was so sore I asked for a heat pack. This helped, but still, I didn't sleep well.

The following day, a doctor came in to put the cannula in. A nurse had done it twice before and I trusted her. She had done it well.

"Ahh!" I couldn't help the sound escaping as the cannula needle went in.

"The vein is bruised," the doctor said.

It kept hurting.

He gave me an antihistamine, and I prayed I wouldn't have any adverse reactions to it. I hoped it would just make me sleep.

The area around the cannula began swelling. I felt worried. Did this mean the next lot would sting. I had to let the nurses know if it did.

In the afternoon, after the nurses did their daily change over the injection site was checked by the new nurse. There was a hard lump there now. The chemo had leaked into the surrounding tissue.

The nurse and I agreed I should try another cannula, so she called for an emergency one to be put in. We were both glad we did, as the next lot of chemo was Doxorubicin Hydrochloride which was nicknamed the *red devil*. If it had leaked into the surrounding tissue, it would've killed the tissue.

The chemo only took six hours this time, which was a lot easier. Afterwards, I overheard a nurse saying I'd be in hospital until Saturday, while my sugars were high. They were normally high for the five days I was taking Prednisolone. I was glad I would be staying in hospital, as I worried about being at home with high sugars. Nothing was done when they were high, so I knew I wouldn't call the hospital even when they were. I wanted to have insulin to bring them down. I hated them being over 15 and they usually went up around 20 before coming down.

During the night, my face began burning again and my neck glands swelled up. I was thankful the swelling didn't affect my breathing like it had the first time. I thought the swelling was less than the previous time as well. However, I did need an injection for fluid retention.

I was also thankful my heart didn't thump as loudly this time either. Had the Lord strengthened my heart according to His promise? I felt a lot better than after the previous lot of chemo.

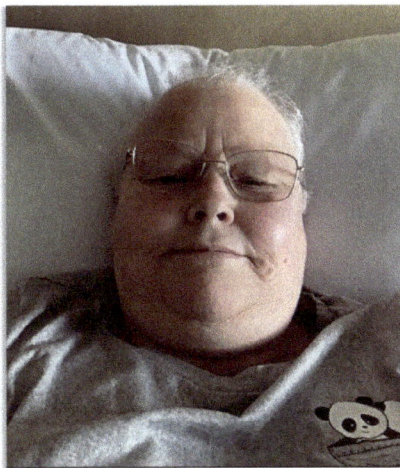
Swollen face on day two of the cycle

The following day when I looked in the mirror, I saw my cheeks were very pale as though I was wearing a mask, with straight lines of red on the side of my face. It was weird. The swelling was receding though, so that was good. My heart began thumping when I got up, so I went back to bed and lay very still. I was glad I was sleepy and dozed off and on most of the day. Maybe the antihistamine had done that. Whatever the cause, I was glad to be able to sleep the painful time away.

When I woke, I prayed for my doctors. For one I prayed that the Lord would protect him as he travelled. I didn't know he had to travel to John Flynn hospital for a clinic, so my prayer was spot on. I told him I'd prayed for him. He said he'd been very busy, and the Gold Coast was getting busier. I agreed.

In my Bible I read, *"The one who offers thanksgiving as his sacrifice, glorifies me."*[24]

---

[24] Psalm 50:23

Sometimes thanksgiving is a hard thing to do, but the following day thanksgiving was in my heart.

Nicola phoned again and we prayed together. She prayed I'd be surrounded by angels and after we'd finished, I was very briefly aware of one and gave thanks to God even though I didn't feel it's ministrations at that time.

I read the Bible verse, *"Gather to me my godly ones who have made a covenant with me by sacrifice."*[25]

I thought of the sacrifice Jesus had made on the cross. By His sacrifice I could gather to Him, and by my thanksgiving He was glorified.

A nurse entered. "Are you still Jennifer Kathleen Phillips," she asked? She had come in to give me an insulin injection, as my sugars had been too high again.

"Yes. That's still me ... maybe I'd be better if it wasn't," I laughed.

I didn't feel the needle go in and worried that it hadn't as the insulin made no difference to the time it took for my sugars to come down. I worried that it might've been a dud one.

The following day the doctor said I was just given a small dose so my sugars wouldn't get too low in the night. If they did, I could become unconsciousness or have a fit.[26]

I was going to go home the following Saturday, but my face, neck and throat were swollen, and sore inside and I was worried about it. I even felt unwell when I was asleep.

Being the weekend, a different doctor came to see me, but she couldn't examine me without a nurse. She said she

---

[25] Psalm 50:5
[26] Hypoglycaemia—commonly called a hypo.

would come back either later in the day, or the following day, to check me out, so I ended up staying another night.

What a terrible night it was. I dreamt I was fighting cancer, which I was of course. I kept waking and moaning and groaning.

The female doctor came back and confirmed throat thrush. I'd never had it this bad.

As she was about to leave, I asked about going home.

"Do you think you can manage?" she asked.

"Yes, I think I can. It's only thrush," I said.

I didn't feel well but thought they would be pleased I was going home, and it was quiet at home.

Peter came and took me home. Rather than unpack my bag like I had previously, I immediately went to bed so my heart wouldn't race and thump as badly as it had in the past. I slept very deeply for two hours and woke without a loud thumping heart. I was very hungry though. Thankfully, Peter had put on a lamb roast, so I had a very big helping.

The following morning, I got up for breakfast then lay down as my heart was thumping heavily again. When it settled, I got up and cleaned my teeth. My heart rate began to speed up again, so I lay down until the thumping stopped. I was then able to get up and have a shower. Afterwards I was so tired I immediately went back to slept.

For the next two days my neutrophils would be at their lowest and I might be anaemic, so I declared the Lord my refuge and protection.

The phone rang. It was my friend Paula. She asked if it was okay to come for a visit. I said yes, even though I didn't have much immunity. The benefit of her visit would outweigh the danger, and I'd already prayed for protection.

Her visit was just what I needed to divert my mind.

By Saturday of the second week, my heart had stopped racing. I was well enough to wash the bathroom floors, but the following day my neck hurt terribly. I tried a hot water bottle and massage. But it didn't help.

Annette Milnes had sent me one of her calendars, so I showed Paula.

Two days later I was fretting. I'd run out of one of the medications I was on, an antibiotic. I needed a script. I didn't have an appointment booked for the doctor. Should I have had one? The first time Doctor Abba had booked a follow-up appointment for me. Was he supposed to initiate them, or was I? I didn't know. I'd been waiting for his receptionist to send a text about the next appointment, but it didn't come. Had the doctor forgotten me? Had I been booked into the hospital for my next lot of chemo or not?

I phoned Dr Abba's practice and was told I was booked in as an outpatient. I told her how unwell I was the day following chemo. She said she'd check with the doctor.

I fretted some more. The Lord lovingly reminded me He was with me, but I was still worried. I prayed for His will in the matter, but the anxiety didn't go away. Maybe it was a side effect of the chemo. I'd never been like this before.

Around midday, the peace of God came into my heart. Later I phoned the pharmacy to see if the script had been sent and it had.

The following day I phoned again and asked for an appointment with the doctor. The receptionist said he was booked out, but she let me know I wasn't booked in as an outpatient. The matter had probably been resolved for me the previous day about mid-day when the peace of God came upon me.

Two days later, even though I didn't feel very well, I had to move some bricks to prepare for the tree remover to remove some yuccas from the front of our property. I moved some in the morning and had to sit down until my heart stopped racing and I was able to breathe normally again. I did the rest in the afternoon, but that evening there was pain in my left arm. I hoped it wasn't my heart. It felt like it could be. I prayed and reminded myself that the Lord would strengthen my heart.

It was the first day of November and I woke hearing the Holy Spirit singing the words to the hymn by Edward Mote (1834), "*On Christ the solid rock I stand. All other ground is sinking sand.*" I love it when this happens. It is very encouraging. A short time later, I heard Him singing again, "*Thy word is a lamp unto my feet and a light unto my path.*" It was the King James Version of Psalm 119:105.

On Thursday the 4th November Peter and I went out to my first church meeting since having chemo. The group that met monthly wasn't a big one so I thought it would be okay. I also felt well enough to go. It was lovely to be social again, and lovely to have people pray for me in person. We also prayed for the church on the Gold Coast to be empowered to share.

On the way home Peter and I both had blood tests. The lady taking my blood asked me about when I'd found out about the cancer, so I told her how I'd gone to hospital after being told to do so by the health line person I'd been talking to. I went to the hospital thinking it was covid, but it turned out to be cancer. I told her how the nurse had offered me medication so I could sleep as she thought I'd be upset. I wasn't. I told her I'd died once before and Jesus had sent me back, so I wasn't worried about it.

The lady taking my blood said something about life journey and I remembered my autobiography. I'd checked my purse before going out, so I knew I had a copy with me.

"This is my journey so far, up to 2012," I said. "Would you like it?"

She looked at the back and said, "You give Jesus the glory. That's good."

It turned out she was a Christian too.

When we got home, I realised it was November, the national novel writing month (NaNoWriMo). I've written novels during this time in the past and felt well enough to begin writing this book. So, our prayer for empowerment to share had been answered rather quickly, at least for me.

My neck was becoming unbearable and when someone asked me what I needed prayer for I said, "My neck."

Two days before my fourth lot of chemo I suddenly felt well again. Even the pain in my neck had gone. My eyes weren't as blurry, and my heart didn't thump. The day after I had episodes of dizziness again but managed to get enough cleaning done in preparation for chemo. I asked my friends on Facebook to pray for the cannula insertion. I didn't want any leaking like the previous time.

Chapter 9 ❧ The Fourth Cycle 8/11/21

Peter and me having lunch in Brisbane

I walked down the oncology ward corridor glancing in at patients as I went. They all looked much worse than I felt. The day before, Peter and I had gone out to celebrate our 44th wedding anniversary and I'd been surprised how well I'd coped. I was a little dizzy but still felt well.

There wasn't much room to dance around the room I'd been assigned to this time, but I stood by the window for a moment enjoying the view. A wide expanse of green grass was dotted with people, and I watched them preparing to practice their sport. It reminded me of the park where Peter had played cricket in the late '70's.

I looked at the artwork on the wall and thought it interesting. Each room had an artwork depicting a beach scene. The order of the rooms I'd been assigned meant that each artwork showed a little more of the sea than the one before. In the first, it had been mostly the beach plants. Now the sea was in full view. What would the next one be like?

I put my things away and prayed the doctor putting the cannula in would do a good job and there'd be no chemo leaking.

He came in and we looked for a vein to use that hadn't been used before. My arm was sensitive, and I was a bit jumpy. He touched me around the site, and I flinched each time. He said I was still sensitive or something like that. I told him a doctor had once told me I was hypersensitive, and there were good and bad things about being like that. I couldn't think what they were right then. I'd forgotten them, so I was glad he didn't ask. Brain fog?

Two nurses came in and each said the cannula looked good. It did. It felt better than the previous one, so that was indeed good. I silently thanked the Lord and prayed it wouldn't leak. The drip started at 1pm. and finished at 7.15pm without leaking.

In the afternoon Doctor Abba visited.

"You're looking good," he said. I was still wearing my wig. It must have been that, as I didn't feel great.

"Thank you, "I said.

He said I'd be in until Saturday. "Only because of the sugars."

I was pleased. I really didn't want to be home when I felt so unwell. I couldn't care for myself and didn't want to overburden Peter.

I told him I thought I should have the insulin when my sugars got to 15 instead of waiting until they got to about 20.

"Haven't they been giving it to you?" he said.

"No."

80

"Do you do scans after the fourth cycle?" I asked. I couldn't wait to see how things were going. The lymph nodes in my groin had felt smaller after the angel had left the room before I'd even started chemo, and I couldn't wait for confirmation. The doctor organised one.

It wasn't such a good night, but the bed was more comfortable than the previous time and the Lord reminded me He was my helper and would help. Medication also helped during the night. I reminded myself and God, (although He has a perfect memory) of His promise in scripture to strengthen my heart. He answered with a large dose of peace.

I was delighted to find my glands didn't swell up as much as they did after the other lots of chemo. They still gave me a very fat face, but they weren't hard.

Doctor Abba arrived very early the next day, and said I was in hospital to rest and so I could be cared for. Something like that. It sounded so lovely. I suddenly felt like I had a deep need to be cared for.

The day before, a nurse had said, "So, what are you in for this time?"

"Chemo. Like last time," I'd said. Didn't she know?

She'd leapt backwards in surprise.

"The doctor wants me in to keep an eye on my sugars," I said.

After that, a chemo sign had been put up on my door ... I wanted to be cared for.

The next day my heart didn't thump loudly, and I only had a mild headache. I was sleepy though. Most days Peter visited me in the afternoon. This day he came in the morning, and I fell asleep while he was visiting. I slept most of the morning. That was a great way to pass day two which was normally the worst day of the cycle.

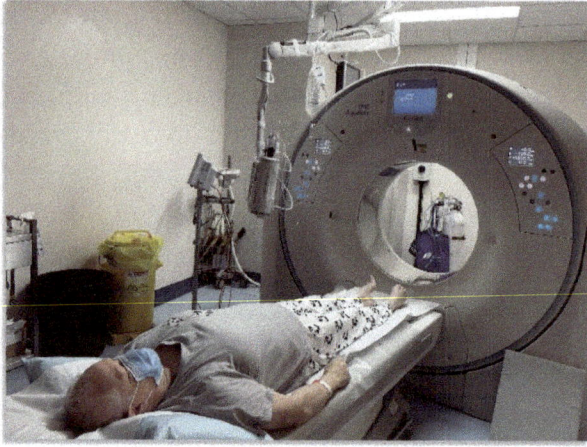

Time for another scan

I was given fast acting insulin before dinner. Doctor Abba had left instructions to give it to me if my sugars reached 15. I was so glad. Apparently, he'd told them to before, but I'd only had it once. I was so glad they were not going to wait until they were higher.

I woke often during the night and didn't feel well. At 4.39am, I read some psalms and prayed. My voice was croaky, but I managed some lines of a few songs. I prayed to be filled with God's love again so Jesus would shine through me, and He did. I could feel the smile in my eyes again. All the following day my mind felt the best it had for a long time.

When Doctor Abba came in, I told him I wasn't afraid of nausea or the dying process anymore but didn't want to be tested on it. I had to chuckle when I got nauseous during the day.

On Thursday 11th November, I went for a scan. The next day, Doctor Abba arrived with some good news. The scan results showed complete resolution in the left pelvis. That was the area I'd felt collapse when I'd seen the doctor's angel before the first lot of chemo. There was only a partial response in the abdomen. That wasn't so good.

The scan report also said the retrocaval lymph node had been associated with some compression of the left renal vein and this hadn't changed since the chemotherapy. Was it median accurate syndrome as the report suggested?

I wondered if the scarring was from another car accident I'd been in. At that time, I'd had wire-like pain right through the sternum, in that very spot. However, it had only been in the last six months or so that I'd had symptoms typical of median accurate syndrome. They included nausea and burning pain in the area. I'd associated pain in that area with my heart.

Doctor Abba thought it might have been scarring. He said I'd have another Pet scan after the 6th cycle and that would show if there was any activity left.

I was still full of questions. Did I need the Lord to send another angel? I remembered the Lord saying to let Him lead me through the chemo, so I decided I needed the chemo too. Were two more cycles going to be enough? I hoped it would be.

The words I'd read the day before in my daily Bible reading interrupted my thoughts. *Anyone who keeps my word will not see death.*[27] I welcomed the change of focus and thanked the Holy Spirit for reminding me.[28]

As I meditated on them, I had a vision of an entity clothed in black. There was light shining down to the ground in front of him. I prayed that the Lord would help me to watch, guard, and keep His word. I wanted the light

---

[27] John 8:51
[28] John 14:26

to be shining down in front of me. I didn't want to be led by dark thoughts.

The thumping headache was back the following day. I managed it with Panadol and sleep.

I went home on the 13th but didn't go straight to bed so ended up with a fast heartbeat again. I slept for half an hour and woke with another thumping head. I took some more Panadol and slept again, which eased it.

In the evening, a strong feeling of anxiety engulfed me. I hadn't been kind enough. I tried to rebuke it. "Help me Lord," I cried.

I fell asleep but my heart felt like it was racing strongly all night. My throat was raging, and I felt like I'd been in a battle with death. I had a very vivid dream. I was participating in a detective type game to find a killer. The word death permeated my sleep, and the spirit of darkness was still in my mind as I woke. I felt terrible. I thought this side effect must be what the doctor meant by the flu like symptoms. Or was it just thrush like the last time I was in hospital. Panadol and sleep had helped throughout the day, but during the night it didn't.

By morning my heart felt a bit better. I felt light and peace around me. At that moment, Barbara, one of the lovely ladies from church, who is always doing good deeds and praying for people, messaged me. She said they had just prayed for me. So, the visitation of light and peace was an answer to their prayers.

I meditated on John 8:51: *Anyone who keeps my word will not see death*. Although it felt like death had been all around me, I was still alive, and I thanked God.

At 6.30am I got up and had some breakfast. Two hours later I took more Panadol, without checking the time.

Suddenly I wondered if I'd had some at breakfast time or not. I couldn't remember. Oh dear! 6.30 felt like an age ago.

The hospital pharmacy had left the thrush tablets out of my discharge medications, so I sucked on a lozenge from the care pack Anna's Lorikeet card-making team had sent me. I was so thankful for them.

As I was enjoying the lozenge, the phone rang. The hospital had finally sorted things out. They'd sent a script to the pharmacy, so Peter was able to get it. Out he went traipsing after me again.

Later, I was well enough to sit up. I put on a mask when two men came to install new blinds in my workroom. I was glad that job was done, as it completed the new art studio. Other jobs around the house were still incomplete. We were still waiting for tradespeople to come and complete the work we'd ordered before I went into hospital.

I began having more nausea. It lasted longer too, but I didn't want to take any more medication or eat to get rid of it. I already felt like a bottle of pills.

Peter was going to Brisbane on Saturday 20th October to have lunch with his brother and sister-in-law. I said I wouldn't go as I wasn't well enough. However, when I woke on the Saturday I felt okay. I hadn't seen them for some time.

I prayed for protection and wore my mask on the train even though I was the only person wearing one. I also had a small bottle of hand sanitiser and used that too.

The train ride didn't seem to take as long as it usually did. I was so pleased I was able to cope. I enjoyed the lunch and had the peace of the Lord. The ride home seemed very quick as well, so that was great.

Going out made it feel like Spring was in my mind, but the following day I was unwell again. I spent most of the day on my bed. My sugars were a little high and the nausea worse, except for a short time after eating. In the evening, I ignored the nausea and worked on this memoir and the following day while praying, the Lord encouraged me with the words, "*Be radiant my bride, for my desire is for you.*"

Alberto who'd come and cleaned the floors for us the day I got out of hospital after the first lot of chemo, came to visit again. He'd made a lasagna for Peter, who couldn't resist sampling it as soon as he left. Alberto let me know of a lady who could help us with the cleaning and gardening. Her name was Eloise. He said she had just started going to our church. She sounded perfect.

The following day we were hit by a thunderstorm just before Eloise arrived so that was the end of the gardening. It worked out for good though, as Eloise got a lot of inside cleaning done. We shared testimonies and experiences, and I was greatly encouraged by her company.

On the 25th November, Peter drove me to the heart centre in Pindara Hospital. I had an appointment with a cardiologist following a Holter monitor test. This was a 24-hour heart monitor.

Before seeing the doctor, a nurse took my details. Although I didn't realise it, I was very tired. I was going through the motions of answering the questions.

"You are from New Zealand," she said.

I was jolted back into the conversation. She took my blood pressure, and that was fine, then did an ECG. She asked about children, and I told her I had three on earth and some in heaven. I told her I'd seen them dancing there. One, who looked a lot like our eldest daughter, had thick blond curly hair and a very angelic face. She was the one who had said, "We are all happy here waiting for you."

The nurse led me to a waiting bay, and I sat beside another lady who was also waiting to see the cardiologist. We chatted before she went in. Then it was my turn.

"Why are you here?" the doctor said, or something to that effect.

I had to think hard. "I've been getting more and more breathless doing less and less," I said. "Some of the conditions I have, have the same symptoms."

I told him about my recent experiences of a racing heart.

"Did you time them?" he asked.

"No." I said. It had never entered my head to do that.

He wasn't too worried about the Holter monitor test results. I told him they were a little worse than the last one I'd had. I couldn't remember when that was. I thought he seemed a little surprised I'd had a previous one. I told him about how hard I'd found it raising my chest to breathe after the last lot of chemo. "It was a bit like when I died in hospital," I said.

He asked about my death experience, and I told him what had happened and what Jesus had done, but it was such an effort to talk. I had to push the words from within. I was finding it difficult to co-ordinate breathing and talking.

He asked about the thumping heart. "Was it thumping or whooshing ..."

Suddenly I couldn't think any more. I was too tired, and my joy flew out the window. It was a very odd experience.

"I don't know," I said, which I regretted saying later. I did know. I could've explained it, but right then I had no thinking energy left. It was just too hard.

He abruptly concluded the appointment. "I'll send you for a CT cardiology angiogram and an echocardiogram," he said.

I hadn't made the most of the appointment. I was thankful I'd reached the medical threshold and so only had to pay 20% of the fee.

I'd had heart tests in the past that showed arrhythmia but then, I hadn't experienced this thumping symptom as bad as it was now. If it wasn't the heart, was it just diabetes?

The following day Peter took me to Mermaid Waters for the angiogram, where I was given a tablet to bring my heart rate down to normal. Shortly after taking the tablet, I stopped being able to hear my heart beating. That was so good. I suddenly felt really well.

I had to wait an hour for the tablet to bring my heart rate down low enough for them to do the angiogram. That meant another long wait for Peter. It would be a long wait before I got the results too, as my follow-up appointment with the cardiologist was in mid-January. As it happened, the results were released on Christmas Eve. There was no heart disease. I was so glad, but I still didn't know why my heart was racing so much.

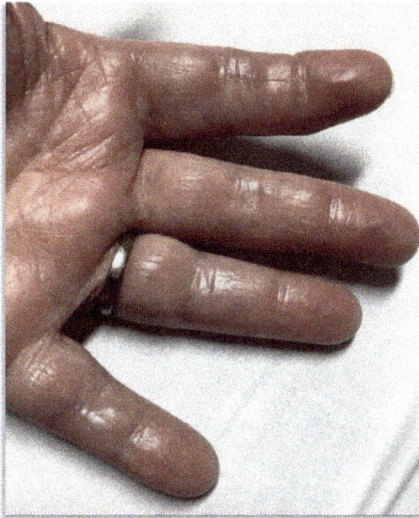

Shiny hands after chemotherapy

I was still terribly tired the day before I was due to have the fifth lot of chemo. I wasn't normally so tired the day before. Yet, as I went into the hospital room, I felt the peace of God with me.

Although it took some time before I realised it, I thought I'd been in this room before. I remembered being opposite the kitchen. There was no mirror in the room. I wasn't used to dental flossing without a mirror, so I used my camera. That worked. I didn't remember doing that before, so maybe it wasn't the same room after all.

The following day, insertion of the cannula was a prolonged painful prick, but the vein wasn't bruised. It looked okay. The nurses even repeated their comments on how good the cannula was and how fast the cannula worked. None had said that before. I was glad.

I'd borrowed an ebook from the library before going to hospital and started reading it. It was called, "*An unconventional wife*," by Mary Hoban. I found it interesting as it depicts life around 1845 in Australia and England, and the rigid expectations for women. The wife, Julia Sorrell didn't fit, nor want to fit the obedient, quiet, submissive model espoused even by her husband. It helped pass the time and I related well to her. I am also a vessel with a difference.

The chemo finished at 9:45pm, taking just over six hours. I was thankful for all those who'd been praying for me, especially that the cannula wouldn't leak. It hadn't.

I'd been told each lot of chemo is worse, but some of the side effects improved each time for me. For instance, my glands were swollen again, but not as much as on day two of the previous cycle. My cheeks were flushed and hot again too but not burning. I was a little nauseous even with anti-nausea tablets, but my heart wasn't thumping loudly and racing. I was very thankful.

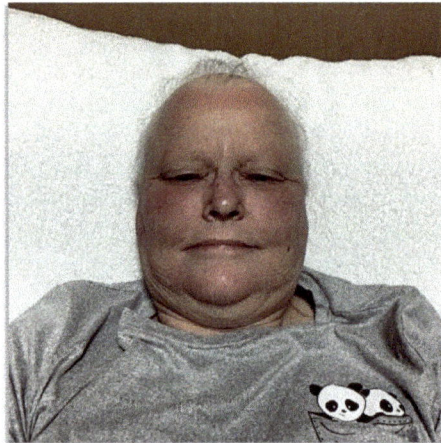

Red halo on forehead

A nurse weighed me and I had put on 2 kilos of fluid overnight. I took a photo and noticed a red halo on my forehead. That made me smile.

I was taken to have a chest X-ray to try and find the cause of my increasing breathlessness. Nothing showed on the X-ray. That was good, but what was causing me to be so breathless?

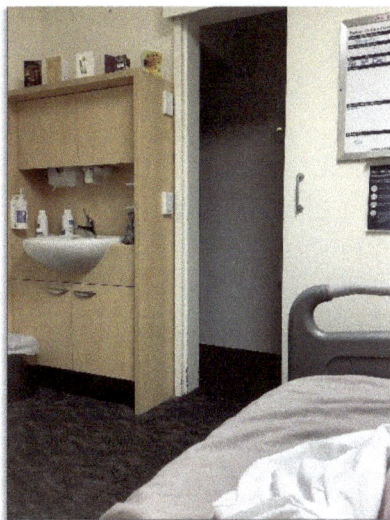
View of cards from my bed

I'd received many cards since starting chemo treatment and they always made me feel so loved. I particularly welcomed them this time. They became the view the room would not have otherwise had.

No matter how sick I am, I've always been able to eat, but that night I couldn't. I was too nauseous. I sat frowning at the food. It looked too bland. I needed to have something because of the insulin I was on, but I just couldn't eat what was in front of me.

A nurse came in.

"I just can't eat it," I said.

"Why not try a little ice-cream?" he said pointing to the ice cream and then the fresh fruit salad.

I picked at it, a little at a time. I could just stomach it. At 11.30pm I managed half a sandwich and had an anti-nausea tablet, but the tablet lasted only an hour.

I slept for two and a half hours that night and a few hours the following day. Even so, it was my best day following chemo. I felt so much better. I still wasn't hungry but was able to eat.

I asked to have the cannula removed early instead of on Thursday or Friday as it had been sore and was bleeding. A nurse took it out. They like patients to have one in for emergencies, but I told her in the past, I hadn't needed it after the chemo, so they didn't put another one in.

As I read the Scripture, *The Lord's hand is not shortened so it cannot save*, I suddenly thought of being saved from cancer.[29] Yes! His hand wasn't too short to do that.

On the other hand, my hands had become shiny.[30] The skin looked thin, glassy and very wrinkled. They felt like they'd been in the water too long. A nurse suggested I take a photo and show the doctor. She took one for me.

When Doctor Abba saw the photo, he pointed out the tightness of the ring. "It's swollen," he said. He rubbed my palm. "Sometimes strange things happen with chemo!"

He gave me the option of going back for the last lot of chemo Monday week, so I'd come out a week before Christmas instead of on Christmas Day.

It felt too soon. "I wouldn't cope," I said.

After he left, I began thinking about it. If I did go in early, I'd be in hospital when our kitchen was out of action due to a renovation, so that would work … but I wouldn't have any recovery time in between. Hmmmm. On the other hand, it would be over a week earlier … what did the Lord want? One week back home? Would that be enough time to recover before the next lot of chemotherapy? I thought I could do it. It would all be over quicker. I yielded myself into God's hands.

---

[29] Isaiah 59:1
[30] Photo on page 89

92

I agreed to what Doctor Abba said, only to find I'd misunderstood him. He meant for me to come in only three days early, on the Friday after the regular blood test, instead of the Monday. That way I'd get out of hospital on the Wednesday, three days before Christmas. That felt better. I agreed to do that.

Six days after the chemo, on the 4th December, I was back home again and went straight to bed. The following night I had a terrible burning stomach. I wanted to sleep through it but couldn't find any sleeping tablets. I thought they must still be at the hospital, so I took a nausea tablet and Panadol, which helped me back to sleep, but the pain was still there in my dreams. I dreamed I should not be having this upset stomach. It kept burning. Yet I was so thankful my throat didn't hurt as much as it had in the previous cycle. My heart wasn't racing all night like previous times either. However, I had two bad nights on day six and seven, instead of one on day six.

I slept a lot the following day, which helped me get through. The words, *"Courage dear heart"* also helped. Melissa (a friend I'd met when I'd travelled to Israel in 2011) had posted them on Facebook. I could hear the love of God in the words. They calmed me.

I was hungry. It's a strange feeling to suddenly feel starving every so often. I was eating more but losing weight. Perhaps it was the fluid from the chemo drip I was losing.

Peter booked in a garden maintenance person, but no-one turned up. He kept contacting them to no avail. Normally it was me fretting, but this time Peter was.

"There are weeds as tall as me," he said.

I was dizzy and kept having low grade fevers, my throat was still sore, and my body dripped sweat. I was in no condition to do it, and Peter wasn't physically able to do it either.

I wanted Peter to stop worrying. "I'll get back into it after the rain and after the chemo stops."

It was day eleven of the fifth cycle. My temperature was 37.7. I took some Panadol, and my temperature came down. I was nauseous, but got up and cleaned the toilets, which made me breathless, so I lay down again. After recovering, I prepared five litres of Roundup and went out spraying some of the most visible weeds down the drive and at the entrance to the property. I thought it would stop Peter from fretting about them. I was breathless again and lay down after a shower. Our children said I shouldn't be spraying. I didn't want to have to do it, but someone had to do it.

Peter also said I shouldn't have sprayed. "I've booked someone to come and give us a quote next week," he said. "They do the house over the road, so they should be reliable."

I was glad someone else was going to do the rest of the spraying. We all thought it was probably the use of the Roundup that had triggered the cancer in the first place. As it turned out, the gardener couldn't start until January.

That week I continued feeling unwell. My stomach was upset, I had abdominal pains, the beginning of a cold sore and my throat and tongue didn't clear up with the thrush medication.

During the third week of my chemo cycle, we had a storm. The wind caused a large tree branch to snap off. I'd often looked at the branch and wanted it removed because it grew out horizontally. The tree grew in the middle of our paddock, so it didn't look safe. I was delighted. The storm had saved me paying for someone to prune it. How funny it looked standing on end, like a digital artwork and concrete poem I'd made and published in *Word Power Poetry & Poetics*.[31] The artwork was based on a blind man in the Bible whom Jesus healed. At first, when Jesus asked him what he saw, he said he saw men as trees. It was as though they were walking.[32] The branch in our paddock looked like a person walking, too.

Fallen branch

We'd decided to change the kitchen benches after two real estate agents had told us the kitchen was old fashioned. At last, the new white marble stone benches with an under-bench basin arrived. The plumber came and I started telling him about what Jesus had said to me, "*Let me lead you through the chemo.*" He asked if I was a Christian. I asked if he was. We both were. I shared some of my experiences of Jesus and gave him my memoir.

I missed social gatherings. In particular, I'd missed going to the Lorikeet Christmas meal Anna put on for demonstrators. However, the ladies sent me heart shaped messages on a string. As I read each one, it filled some of my need for social contract. I felt truly blessed. I hung them where I could see them, and they stayed there for some years as a reminder of their friendship.

---

[31] (Phillips, 2012)
[32] Mark 8:24

The day before I was due to go back into hospital for what I hoped was my last lot of chemo, I invited a few friends for morning tea. It was so good having something else to focus on, although Eloise did lay hands on me and pray for my healing as my hip was aching. I prayed too and had a vision of a white fence. At the time, the vision reminded me of a dream I'd had in November. Its message was, *"Open the gate so the sheep can follow the shepherd. Blow the horn to gather the sheep and worship in the Spirit with gladness."*

In a limited sense, this was what we were doing when we gathered. However, while editing this book I thought, *"What are fences for?"* I'd seen one pure white fence in the vision, not fences and gates. I realised then the fence had been a reminder that the Lord was there with us as our protector.

Trees Walking (2010)

Chapter 11 ⊱ The Sixth Cycle 17/12/21

A selfie to show my wig and the view from my hospital room

The nurses suggested I go into hospital early for the sixth lot of chemotherapy so we wouldn't finish so late at night. So, Peter dropped me off an hour earlier on the 17th December 2021.

For my past hospital stays, someone had escorted me to my room. This time no-one was available. I easily found my way to the room I'd been allocated even though it wasn't one I'd been in before. I opened the wardrobe and felt pleased. It was spacious and my cabin bag fitted easily inside. I noted the mirror and grinned. This was better than last time. The full width windows let a lot of light in and added cheer. They framed the trees that also framed the park.

I turned my back to the view and checked out the pictures on the wall. Were they significant? There were two.

One was of rocks on a misty beach, the other a beach at sunset. I hoped this was the sunset for the chemo and cancer.

I'd been meditating on Psalm 34:19: *Many are the afflictions of the righteous, but the Lord delivers him out of them all.* I knew I'd see another deliverance, but would it be to this world or the next?

The cannula went in okay. There were no dramas. A little blood escaped but there wasn't any other leaking.

The chemo started at 12.50pm and finished at 7.50pm. It went so quickly this time because I fell asleep during the afternoon. High sugar levels often cause me to fall asleep. My sugars were higher this time because I'd remembered to take the Prednisolone at breakfast and not with lunch, when I got into hospital.

Looking back, the months of chemo had just zapped away. I was glad and hoped it was the last lot.

That night, I got two hours sleep with the help of a sleeping tablet. I was woken by a nurse. She checked my blood pressure and temperature. I lay awake until after 4am.

When I finally went back to sleep, I dreamt of two fish in a container that was too small with not enough water, so I put them into a larger bowl. Then the fish shop owner prepared a large fish tank with weed and everything they needed. It was a similar dream message to the one I'd had where the sheep were fenced in and needed the gates opened, so they could follow the Shepherd. I wrote it on my Facebook page and hoped whoever the Lord intended this message for, would read it.

When I woke the following day, I checked my glands. It was swollen glands day! However, again they weren't as big as the previous time, and my cheeks weren't burning as much as in previous cycles. Again, that was something to praise God for. However, I still needed Panadol for them.

I asked for an extra nausea injection, as the one I'd had with the drip the day before, hadn't worked. It was

Swollen face on day two again

supposed to last three days. I felt very unwell and sleepy. I told myself I just couldn't go through any more chemo.

I told the Lord I didn't want to go through anymore. I kept repeating it to myself then remembered someone's Facebook post. *We are warriors.* I used this word as a sword instead of repeating what I couldn't face. I could only say it weakly, but it helped divert my mind. Then I declared the Scripture, *"I can do all things through Christ who empowers me."*[33]

That night the Lord said, *"There is work to do,"* so it looked like I did have a future. He let me know He wanted me to pray for someone that night. The following day I found out about the situation I'd prayed for. I hadn't known about it before praying. It was now resolved.

A sleeping tablet let me sleep for two hours again. I was woken at 5.30am by the nurse. I dozed until breakfast and woke feeling as though it was the best night's sleep I'd had

---

[33] Philippians 4:13

in hospital since starting the chemo. However, it didn't do much for my stomach. It was really upset all day.

On Monday, day 4, I woke moaning. There was a knock on the door. I couldn't speak, just mumbled. "Mmm?" I meant come in.

It was Doctor Abba, early as was his habit. He turned the light on, and I reacted. I couldn't bear the light. He noticed and turned it off. I turned on the one behind me. I didn't feel well.

"I wasn't very well yesterday," I said.

He sat down. "What was wrong?"

My mind was a blank fog. "I can't remember," I said. I tried hard and remembered I'd felt very unwell. I'd dry retched. No, that was the day before, or the day before that. My memory had gone.

"Hopefully this is the last lot," Doctor Abba said, or something to that effect.

"I can't go through any more chemo," I moaned.

I felt lousy all day, and a new rash appeared on my abdomen. Yet even though I felt so lousy, I had another divine appointment. That's often the way. God turns our difficult times into blessings.

The divine appointment was with a nurse who had changed wards after twenty years on surgical. She said she was nervous about being in the oncology ward.

As we talked, we discovered some things in common. She was a New Zealander and we'd both lived in Hokitika. I told her I'd had a near drowning there as a little child.

I was about four. Our father had taken us to the beach where he put three or four of us on an inflatable. However, a wave swamped us, and we fell into the sea. I was caught underneath the inflatable. I tried to push it up to breathe, but I couldn't. I panicked. I needed air.

Suddenly I knew what to do. I had to swim sideways to get out from under the inflatable instead of trying to push it upwards. I didn't think I had enough air in my lungs to do it, but I tried. I know the peace of the Holy Spirit's voice and wisdom now, but I didn't know it was Him back then. I came up out of the water and was so angry with my father.

"You didn't save me," I shouted.

He'd had to save the baby who couldn't swim, he said. We could swim.

I had nightmares for many years afterwards. I told the nurse how Jesus had delivered me from them. As an adult, I'd asked God to deliver me from all my fears and God began answering my prayer. One way He did this was through a vivid dream. In the dream, I was drowning. I felt the same terror I felt under the inflatable. I had no air left, but suddenly I found I was breathing normally. I was able to breathe under the water! That was the last time I had that nightmare.

I offered the nurse my memoir. She said over the years she's been given a few on the ward and all from New Zealanders. That was amazing.

After she left, I thought of what God had said about there being work to do and remembered a song I'd written years ago. "... *there is work to do sharing the love of Jesus. To make known His name to share His fame ...*" I was glad that even on my worst day, I was able to be about my Father's business.

During afternoon tea I found a heart shaped chip in the packet. It reminded me of God's love for me. It encouraged me again.

The following day the words of a song spoke to me, and I affirmed them, *"If I'm poor. If I'm unwell, here I am. Send me. Let my life reflect how much I love you."*[34] I thought, *"Let it also reflect how much You Lord, love me."*

I had an apple, and my blood sugars were 20.9, the highest recording I'd had. It worried me. What if ...

I left the window open a little, not listening to the thought that insects would come in. I was too weary to get up and close it. A fly came in. That gave me the motivation I needed. I closed the window and swatted the fly. I saw a parable in the incident.

Jesus didn't want to be crucified but He went down that path for us. Our path can be difficult too, but not TOO difficult, if we walk it knowing God is with us. He was with me as He'd promised me. There are battles, and some swatting to do, but the Lord was my deliverer. He would deliver me from all my afflictions, all my troubles as He said He would.

I closed the window to a worry I'd let into my mind. Today's troubles were enough without worrying about what ifs. God is so good. He restored my soul again.

The following morning, I told Doctor Abba that Day six was my worst day. Normally I had a terrible night with a burning stomach, terrible nausea and sore throat. I was even dreading it. I kept praying it wouldn't be as bad as the previous two times. I didn't want to feel as though I was battling death. Doctor Abba said I needed to rest up. I hoped that was the last of the chemo.

---

[34] (Lake et al., 2021)

Chapter 12 ◆ Christmas in Hospital

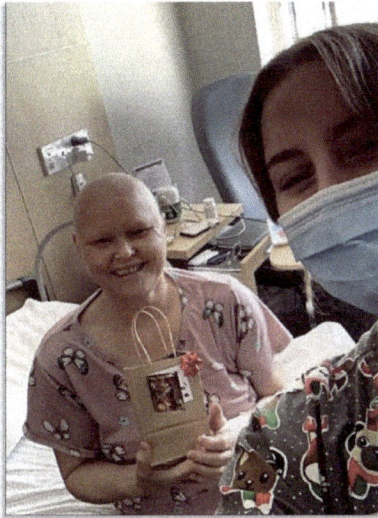

A present from the hospital staff

On the 22nd December, I was anxious. I recognized the pattern of side effects. It was the fifth day of the cycle, the day when anxiety was the strongest. I went home, but the gastro gel wasn't among my meds, nor was my Thyroxine. I phoned the hospital, and a nurse phoned back. She said she didn't live too far from me, so she'd drop them off on her way home. I was glad she came. I desperately needed the gel as the worst night of the chemo cycle was upon me.

It was bad. I had strong bone pain, racing heart, and a bloated abdomen, which I'd never had before. I also had a headache, and a burning stomach.

I had strange dreams too. One seemed prophetic. I thought its message was about a person who wanted the scriptures but not the Holy Spirit.

The words, "Here I am Lord send me … I love you Lord," kept wafting through my head.[35] It sounded like an angel was singing in my mind. My heart sang the words too, but I didn't have the strength to audibly sing them.

The following day, Day 7, I had another fever. My temperature was 38.2 Celsius, I hadn't felt well all day. I phoned Amanda, my chemo navigator.

"I don't want to go back into hospital," I said. "It might come down."

Amanda suggested taking my temperature in an hour, which I did. I also took some Panadol, which usually brought my temperature down. This time it didn't. My temperature had gone up a fraction. It was 38.3 Celsius. I tested it with two different thermometers to make sure and took photos of the readings.

Peter voiced his anxiety, but after another phone call to Amanda, he relaxed, and we headed back to the hospital.

I showed the first doctor my photo. "I have a fever," I said.

She took my temperature. It was back in the normal range.

"I should have waited," I said to her.

"When did you take the Panadol?" She asked.

"About an hour and a half ago," I said.

"That would do it," she said.

I was taken to a bed in the emergency room where my blood pressure was taken. It was 181/77. They did an ECG. I don't know what that showed. My blood sugars were high. I'd had fried rice less than two hours before. Blood tests were also done, and a urine sample taken. The blood test results showed I had an infection. There were white blood

---

[35] (Lake et al., 2021)

cells in the urine, but the doctor thought it may have been cross contaminated. Neither the doctor nor I knew what the infection could be from. I thought it could be a urinary tract infection, but I didn't have many symptoms of one. I pointed to my neck. "It could be my oesophagus." It was still sore, and it was hard to swallow food.

"It's a hospital acquired infection," he said as he looked at a report.

"How did I get that?"

He waved his hands saying something to the effect that where sick people were, infections could be picked up.

Later I read my pathology report, and everything was very low. I had macrocytic, decreased platelets, anaemia, moderate thrombocytopenia, toxic granulation and dohle bodies, which suggested infection or sepsis. The neutrophils and lymph's were also low, as well as other things.

I was taken to the oncology ward again and was told I'd been given a nice room, because it was probably my last time. An antibiotic was administered via a drip and anti-nausea medication as well.

I dreamt a large billowing grey cloud was blowing on a man. He stood firm against it, but his wife cowered behind him. The man was shining and full of joy. Then the cloud saw me and came after me. I told everyone to shut the doors, but we didn't get them shut in time. The storm cloud began to blow at me through the door. I closed my eyes and began declaring, "I am a servant of the Lord. I am a prophet of the Lord. Stop your blowing. Be still." I opened my eyes, and it was gone. I asked if anyone had seen it go.

I woke up. A nurse came in to check on me. It was 3.30am. I had a low-grade fever, so the room temperature was turned down, and then I got too cold.

I was looking forward to the second lot of antibiotics. It was Christmas Eve and around 6.30am, a nurse came in and set the drip up. She began the saline flush, but it stung too much. I could see a small swelling at the cannula site.

"The doctor who put this in said the vein was bruised," I said. "He should just have put in another one."

The nurse checked the site. "We'll have to take this one out. I'll put in an order for another one," she said.

The morning passed and I waited eagerly for the new cannula, but no-one arrived to do it. The staff changed and still no doctor arrived to do the job. I let the new staff know it hadn't been done.

Around mid-day I saw a man in a blue uniform looking at my folder on a trolley by the door. At last, it was a doctor to put in a new cannula.

"I've been hanging out for you," I said. I liked the first dose of antibiotic. I had felt mildly better after the drip and wanted more.

He motioned to the side of the bed. "May I sit here?"

"Yes," I said.

He took my hand and held it firmly, turning it over. I pointed out the bruise and spots at the previous site. He turned my arm over, tapping my wrist with two fingers. I jerked it back in horror, but he held it firm.

"Ah! It's bruised. It hurts." Why did I say it was bruised? I couldn't see one, but it sure felt like it was when he tapped it.

He raised his hand as though he was going to tap it again. My whole body reacted in terror. I automatically tried to jerk my arm away again, but he held it firm in his hand, all the time watching my face closely. Was he teasing me? He didn't look as though he was joking. Had he seen an abnormal reflex action, like the Babinski reflex?[36]

"Not there," I pleaded. "There's a lump,"

He rubbed the lump with his finger then looked for another possible site on the back of my hand. I didn't want it there either.

"That's the most painful place," I said, but let him carry on.

He put the cannula in the back of my hand, and it didn't hurt as much as I remembered. The vein was viable.

While chatting, I mentioned I had an infection.

Pointing to the drip on the stand he said, "Is that what that's for?"

"Yes. They don't know what the infection is. It could be a urinary tract infection or ..." I pointed to my neck where it hurt.

He leaned forward startled. "Is it Covid?"

"No," I said. "I haven't been anywhere to get it."

I'd been home and then back to hospital ... I remembered the supermarket. On the way home from hospital, we'd stopped at the supermarket and for the first time since I'd been diagnosed, I'd gone in with Peter to get a few Christmas things. There was hardly anyone in the store. I was surprised at the time. Anyway, that was only yesterday and surely, Covid would've shown up in my blood test the night before if I'd had it. Surely, they would've tested me for that then. No, I didn't have the symptoms.

---

[36] Toes point upwards instead of downwards when foot is stimulated.

"You only need to be in Queensland," he said and left quickly. At the door, he turned before checking my notes. "Merry Christmas for tomorrow."

"Thank you. Have a refreshing Christmas," I said.

It wasn't the best day. I felt like moaning and groaning most of the day.

That night I dreamt I was walking in a land of ice. It felt so real. I woke with terrible

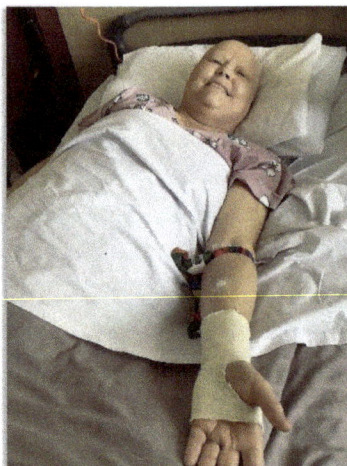

Christmas morning blood test

coldness right inside my head. It was so cold it hurt. I began moaning trying to get out of the pain and terror of it. I pulled the blankets up to warm my body, but it didn't help. The pain in my head was really strong. I pressed the buzzer for the nurse, got up, turned the air conditioner off and lay down again. I felt warmth coming back into my head. The nurse arrived and I asked for Panadol.

"Do you have a headache," she asked?

"Yes, a really bad one," I said.

She gave me the Panadol.

I went back to sleep and woke up on Christmas morning.

"A Christmas present from Doctor Abba," the pathologist said as he entered the room. He smiled as he proceeded to take some blood.

I laughed.

I had more anti-nausea medication via the drip and later that morning some of the staff appeared with a present. It included just what a chemo patient needed, moisturising cream. It was such a lovely gesture. It made me feel like it *was* actually Christmas day.

Peter arrived in time for afternoon tea. I was so appreciative of him driving back and forth every day to visit me. It took out a big chunk of his day. I was glad he was allowed to have a cuppa with me too, especially this day as the cakes had been beautifully decorated. They looked too nice to eat.

Christmas afternoon tea with Peter

I had more anti-nausea medication so I could enjoy the Christmas dinner and video meetings with family that took up much of the rest of the day.

On Boxing Day, I was due to go home. The weekend doctor came and said I was the brightest she'd ever seen me. I did feel so much better. No nausea that morning and I wasn't feeling like sleeping all the time.

"I think I've had an infection every cycle, only I thought it was just the chemo," I said.

"Chemo is blamed for a lot of things," she said.

She ordered another blood test, and I came off the antibiotic drip and onto a powerful oral antibiotic, on top of the other three I'd been taking to protect me since starting the chemo.

By lunchtime, I wasn't feeling so good again. My neck, jaw and head began to hurt. I began thinking I shouldn't be going home, but I just lay there. The pain became severe. I asked and received Palexia, instead of Panadol.

The blood test came back. Everything was still very low but improving. -anaemia, moderate toxic granulation and dohle bodies, low platelets neutrophils and lymph's, etc. Still, the doctor was happy for me to go home. At least at home, I wouldn't be acquiring more hospital acquired

At home after Christmas

infections. I'd be able to eat the Christmas feast our children had ordered for us and Peter wouldn't have to drive all the way to see me each day.

Peter came to take me home. When I opened the car door there was a bunch of lilies he'd bought me. A bouquet of wonder engulfed me.

At home, I had a sleep and woke with a bad headache, nausea and jaw pain again. I checked my temperature. It was 37.7, another low-grade fever. I was disappointed.

I phoned my chemo navigator.

"I'm not running back to the hospital," I said. "No," she said and suggested I keep monitoring my temperature and keep up with the Panadol. "Call an ambulance if your well-being does a nose-dive."

Over the next few days, I continued to have low grade fevers with neck and jaw pains and feeling unwell. Often, they came in the late afternoon, which I discovered was when a person's cortisol levels were lower. I rebuked the fevers and took Panadol and rested. It was always too late to phone my chemo navigator. If I got up for long, I would begin to feel unwell. My neck would start hurting, my heart would race, and my temperature would go up. Once I was too tired to take a Panadol, but my temperature came down just by rebuking it, and with prayer from Facebook friends and of course, rest. However, I didn't like the neck pain so kept taking Panadol to alleviate it too.

Two days after Christmas I was still sleepy. I tried to watch TV in the afternoon but fell asleep. Before bed, I sat with the Lord and read a few psalms. I declared a promise of God again, *"Many are the afflictions of the righteous, but the LORD delivers him out of them all."*[37]

The following day I felt as though I'd turned the corner; however, I began to feel unwell in the afternoon again. I had a mild headache, and the jaw and neck pains were back again too. I checked my temperature, and I had a fever. I went back to bed and the symptoms gradually went away. My temperature went down to 37.3.

On New Years Eve, I really wanted to know if I was healed of cancer. I asked the Lord and fell into a deep sleep, while listening to my favourite songs on Spotify. I woke suddenly to Kristian Stanfill and Passion singing, *"I am healed. I am whole,"* in the song, *"God. You're so good"* (2018).

A little hope rose in my heart. Until then, I hadn't any hope that all the cancer was in remission. I kept thinking I might need another angel visit. Now I began to think I might be healed.

Each day as I looked through the window, out over the orchard, there was so much gardening and harvesting to do.

---

[37] Psalm 34:19

The lychee needed picking. I didn't want them rotting on the ground. There was an extra big lot this year.

On the first day of the third week of the cycle, I decided to pick them. By the time I got to the bottom of the steps I was becoming breathless, so I couldn't pick the tomatoes on the way down.

Bruising from walking into a wing wall

I stopped at the bottom of the steps and looked at the bay tree. Half the bay tree was diseased, and my fig tree didn't look good either. It looked like it was full of disease too.

I found a ripe fig that wasn't being eaten by ants and continued to the lychee tree. I picked as many as I could before becoming too breathless. There was dull pain and tightness in my chest right through to the back. I stopped to try and catch my breath, but it had gone. I didn't think I'd get back up the steps, yet I put one foot after the other slowly stopping here and there. I felt as though I was about to have a heart attack, but I did it! I got back up the steps.

I reminded my-self my heart had no disease according to the recent angiogram. Was it a lack of oxygen from anaemia? I was still very pale. I cried out to the Lord to help me.

Eventually I got back to my bed and lay there. The exercise had caused my temperature to go up to 37.3. I was thankful it fell short of a low-grade fever. I lay there most of the rest of the day, exhausted. My upper body muscles felt as though they'd had a workout.

On the 5th January, I had breakfast just before 4am because I had to fast for a PET scan. I turned the lights out and started back to bed but walked straight into a wing wall. It badly bruised my eyebrow and was extremely sore.

I hadn't walked into a wall since I'd had a brain injury in a car accident in 1997. At that time, I was always misjudging distances and missed seeing the edge of walls. I would head in the direction of where I wanted to go and hit a wall if it happened to be in the way. Doorways seemed too small as well and I often bumped against an edge. I learned to put my hand on the door frame before entering.

During the previous PET scan, the noises had made me want to laugh. A few times I had. I was supposed to stay very still. It had been so hard to control myself. So for this one, I asked the Lord to help me not to laugh. He did.

During the scan my arms had to stay still in an unbearable position. They ached so much I didn't even notice the noises and certainly didn't feel like laughing.

The following day at my appointment with Doctor Abba, he told me I was in complete metabolic remission. I should've been over the moon, but I still wasn't feeling well. I had a headache and swelling where I'd walked into the wall.

"There is one area that is still enlarged," Doctor Abba said. He thought it might be scarring. The PET scan report he gave me said it was about 10 times smaller than it had been, and there was no avid activity.

I was a little concerned when he told me I had a possible 11mm meningioma adjacent to the right frontal bone in my head, which needed keeping an eye on. It hadn't been reported in any scans before.

I asked how an eye would be kept on it. Doctor Abba said he'd organise another scan when I saw him in April. That was three months away. In the meantime, I needed to stay away from groups until February at which time I would've had my Covid booster shot, and my immunity would be stronger.

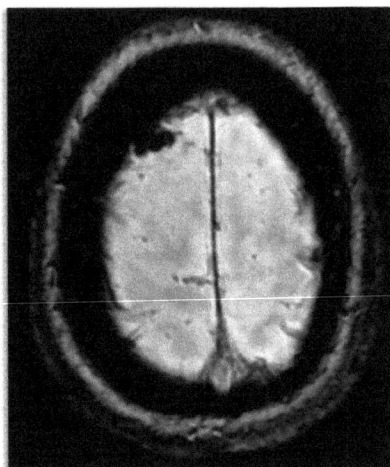

Brain scan showing meningioma before it was reported (July 2021)

I continued having a continuous bad headache on the left side, where I'd walked into the wall. It lasted for about three weeks, then it improved a bit. My GP sent me for an MRI, but thankfully, it didn't show any late bleeding. The continuous headache stopped, and I just had occasional headaches for a year or so after that.

I was curious about meningioma's, and a card-making friend told me she'd had one. She gave me a support group to join on Facebook. I did, but everyone's stories were too scary for me. I wasn't ready to face anything else. I decided I needed to rejoice in the lymphoma remission and forget about a possible brain tumour. I should be rejoicing in the healing.

"I am healed," I said out loud and smiled. "I am healed."

Chapter 13 ✦ One Thing After Another

On the 11th January 2022, I was terribly tired, so I checked my sugars. They were too high. I asked my friends on Facebook to pray and went outside to try, through exercise, to bring the sugars down. I trimmed part of a hedge, had lunch then fell into a deep sleep. I woke without the terrible tiredness that sometimes accompanied high sugars, so I went outside and continued trimming until I disturbed a nest of wasps and was stung.

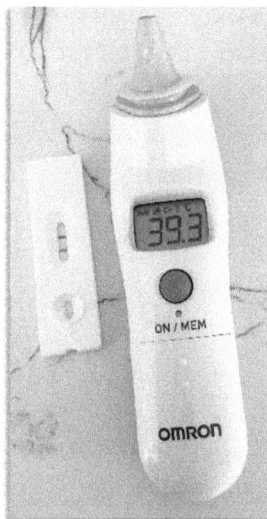

The following day, I woke up, and movement made me dizzier than I'd been before. Even nodding at something Peter said, while sitting, brought it on. I decided I had to change what I'd been having for breakfast – go back to what I used to have before chemo.

A smaller breakfast wasn't satisfying and by 9am I was feeling hungry, which meant I needed to have something for morning tea. To deal with the extra sugars, I would just have to go outside again and continue trimming the hedge. I'd leave the area where the wasp nest was. Hopefully I'd finish the hedge, but I was tired. I procrastinated.

I'd looked up brain tumour symptoms. I certainly had been having some. I'd recognised brain injury symptoms before and during chemo and put it down to lymphoma and the brain fog that came with chemo. Irritability, cognitive issues, dizziness, fatigue, headaches, slurry speech … What was I thinking? I wasn't going to think about it. I needed to put it out of my mind. I needed to focus on Jesus.

Thank you, Jesus, for healing me from lymphoma.

I went outside and trimmed more of the hedge. I was so glad I did, as I discovered some ripe elderberries the birds hadn't eaten, and one ripe fig. I swiped at some of the weeds that were nearly as tall as I was before I was too breathless to continue.

When I got back up the steps, I took one glove off and put two pieces of glass I'd found into the bin. I went to take the other glove off as well, but it wasn't on my hand. That was odd. I looked in the bin in case it had accidentally fallen in. It hadn't. I retraced my steps and found it. I must've taken one off without realising it, or forgotten I had.

I checked my sugar levels. Yay! They were only 6.8. I was a bit shaky, but going back to my old breakfast had worked, that and the few minutes of exercise. This meant I could eat a sugar free muffin I'd made. It was a new recipe I'd created, and I liked it. Each time I made them they were different depending on what suitable ingredients I found in the fridge or pantry. I'd used an old packet of cherries and some stewed Nashi pears in this one, along with a few small pieces of dried pear.

A week later, I noticed I was sleeping through the night. I hadn't done that for many years. I was still taking Panadol for daily headaches, but was able to do more around the house, inside and out.

My immunity was still low, well below the normal range, and I got a bad cold sore, and a Covid-like flu with low grade fevers off and on. I woke every morning feeling under the weather, and arthritic. I was discouraged and thought the pain in my neck and back would never go away. I rebuked the discouraging thoughts. The enemy was trying to come in through the backdoor of pain, just like in a dream I'd had.

On the 24th January, Peter asked me if I was feeling any better. I didn't have my glasses on and accidentally took oxycodone instead of a cough mixture in the night. It worked better than the cough mixture, but I kept waking mildly itchy all over. I'm allergic to it. It made me feel warmly relaxed though, instead of stiff and arthritic. I was still dizzy, but mildly happy as well.

I woke up on the 26th January and I wasn't crippled with back pain. That was so good. I was also encouraged by a book I was reading. In it a man was in a hopeless situation, one that humanly speaking was impossible to overcome. But he did. God still had a future for him, and I knew God still had a future for me. Hope returned.

In 2020 I'd bought four magnolia trees and on the first day of March 2022, I was finally strong enough to dig the last hole. Although the rain had softened the soil, I wasn't strong enough to dig it in one go, but I did finally finish it. Sadly, the magnolias all died. Our climate wasn't the best for them.

It was one thing after another. No sooner had I recovered from the flu than I got another infection with boils. No wonder I'd been so tired. The upside to that was the antibiotic made the pain on the left side of my head go away for a while. However, it didn't get rid of the boil. I ended up with two. I was so tired, and the headaches kept me on my bed. I used the time to listen to sermons, so I'd keep a positive attitude.

I went to the haematologist for my three-month post chemo check. My blood test showed I was still immuno-compromised from the lymphoma, and I hadn't developed any antibodies or immunity to covid despite 4 vaccinations.

So, the doctor applied to the state government for me to get the Evusheld vaccination, which is two injections, one of Cilgavimab and the other Tixagevimab. He said I still needed to wear my mask and stay away from large groups until after these injections.

I went for a blood test and had one good reading. Only twice before my GP had seen my sugars as low as they were. I'd been feeling like I didn't have diabetes so that was good. However, my blood pressure wasn't. My GP wanted me to check it at home, so I bought a monitor.

On the 6th April 2022, my blood pressure was too high: 205/102. I phoned the Health Line and was told to go to the hospital. I spent a couple of days in the hospital where my blood pressure was monitored, and my medication changed.

A couple of days after being discharged my blood pressure was high again, so I spent the day lying down. It was 214/93. I'd had earache the day before as well, so I left a message for my GP.

Four days later I got an appointment with her. She asked if my ear hurt and when she touched it, I jumped with pain, but on inspection no infection was seen. My blood pressure had improved slightly. It was no longer in the seek urgent medical attention range but seek medical attention. So, she said to stop monitoring it until a week before my next appointment in May.

The following day the throbbing in my ear stopped, although it was still a little sore. I rested in the morning and felt well enough to make some gluten free Afghans. After lunch I felt well enough to do some chain sawing. I finished cutting down a mulberry tree whose fruit only grew to the size of my little finger. I'd had it since it was a tiny self-sown plant hoping it would produce good fruit. It didn't. Each year I hoped but now it was just taking up space in our garden and making extra pruning work for me.

After a rest I did some more urgent pruning with the chainsaw. I was too tired to finish the job. I just

My sister Kath and I making Christmas tags

had to leave the pruning's where they fell, but I was glad to be able to start it.

I was missing the social contact I'd been used to again, so I went to see my friend Paula. We spent the afternoon and evening together. During that time, we made a card each, had a meal and watched a Van Gogh DVD. It was such a pleasant time together.

A few days later my sister Kath flew in to visit me, so I had more social contact. She helped me with the tags I was making for hampers for the needy. There were a few hundred, so I greatly appreciated her help.

While she was staying, our daughter Natalie also visited, and we met up with Peter's brother and sister-in-law for a pre-birthday celebration. Not all family members could come for the party I was organising, because of Covid, but I arranged another small morning tea when they were well, and able to visit.

We invited only a few friends, for the actual day because I was immunocompromised, and that was manageable as well. So, my need for social contact was well and truly satisfied.

At my next GP appointment on the 1st of May, I failed the balance test, so an appointment was made with a neurologist, who could also check the meningioma. I was given a new blood pressure tablet to try and that seemed to work. My first reading after taking it was over 55 points lower than the previous one. It was the lowest reading I'd had since buying the blood pressure monitor.

On the 4th May I dropped a heavy long-armed pruning tool on my foot. It cut right through the nail. Black blood oozed out meaning a vein was cut. It was so sore. I thought I'd broken my toe. However, I didn't immediately go to the doctor. It was Peter's day for the car, and I didn't want to ask him to drive me to the doctor. That would mean he'd have to wait again and miss his ukulele meeting.

The following day I did ask him. We were driving home from church, and I suggested we stop at the doctors. I was glad I did as the doctor spoke sternly saying I should have gone in when it happened.

"I might have been able to stitch it," he said. Now he couldn't.

The doctor thought it was already showing signs of infection. I'd thought my symptoms were another bout of thrush coming on, but it was an infection in the toe. So, another antibiotic on top of the three I was already taking every day. I still didn't have much immunity to fight infections. It ended up being another forced period of rest!

On the 6th May I had a visitor. I thought she was my new neighbour whom I'd only spoken to twice. She had the same hair colour, so I invited her in. She came with two bottles of mulled juice.

Half-way through the conversation I realised she wasn't my new neighbour, and I began wondering who she was. It was the third time since chemo I'd missed recognising a person at my door. Chemo brain!

It turned out she was a prophetic artist, as was I. We were among the Christian artists from

Live artist for 2018 Commonwealth Games

Australia who'd been invited to showcase our art in different venues around the city, during the 2018 Commonwealth Games. We'd met during the event. The venue I'd been allocated to paint at was the Australia Fair shopping mall. What a lovely surprise.

In May two friends, Paula and Marilyn, surprised me with lunch out to celebrate my birthday. At the café, the milk jug looked as though it was upside down. I knew I had to tilt the milk jug for the milk to go into the teacup, but I tipped it completely upside down and milk went everywhere. That was very odd.

A real-estate agent contacted us, and I began preparing for his visit. As I did, I began to worry.

"Wait a bit," the Holy Spirit said.

So, I relaxed.

A few years back when we'd been thinking of selling our house, the Holy Spirit had said not to at that time as we'd be here a while. We'd wondered how long a *while* was.

Obviously, it wasn't up yet, so, we decided to continue fixing things that needed doing.

After not having the strength to keep the gardening up for a year or so, I'd paid for help, and now I thought it was finally under control. Although one thing that still needed doing was the shed roof. The gutters were filled with leaves, and a small tree was beginning to grow among them.

On June 15th I woke up dizzy again. However, by late afternoon the dizziness had left so I was able to climb a ladder and clean the worst of the gutter.

I had a lot of art works stored in the garage, and as part of our preparation for putting the house of the market, I decided to get rid of some. It just so happened that a charity, New Hope Care in Brisbane, was wanting art works to sell. I donated 10 artworks for their fundraiser and that decluttered the garage a bit.[38]

When I woke on July 2nd, I was feeling weak, so I began to pray for strength. I had a vision of a volcano. There was a large ball of smoke near the top. It reminded me of an artwork I'd made in 2020. At that time, the Lord was saying, to arise and see things from a high perspective, a heavenly one. We were called to be more like a dynamic volcano than a fragile static glass vessel, which I'd started painting.[39]

As I meditated on this and the volcano vision, I remembered I had the power of the Holy Spirit within me and that was dynamite power, the strength I needed. I stopped letting the thoughts of tiredness rule my actions. I was a volcano. I would follow the Holy Spirit's guidance and take the high view.

---

[38] A picture of the artworks can be seen on page 154.
[39] Page 148

A High Perspective (2020)

That same month I went to the first big church event I'd been to since having cancer. I'd forgotten what the haematologist had said about staying away from large groups until after I'd had the Evusheld vaccination. I wore my mask except when I was eating. A child kept coughing behind me, so I moved to the opposite side of the room. But it turned out to be too late. I developed a sore throat, and a rash appeared on my stomach.

On the 12th July I was extremely sleepy during the night but kept being woken by abdominal convulsions. They caused my body to involuntarily double over. I was so unwell all night I didn't realised what was happening. It wasn't until morning that I remembered our grandson had had convulsions when he caught covid. He had two other viruses at the same time. Our daughter had videoed him and messaged them to me. I had the same sort of involuntary body movements.

In the morning, I did a Rapid Covid test. It was positive. I had Covid! I didn't panic because the Holy Spirit was encouraging me to keep a *positive* attitude. I could hear Him singing a song in my mind, "*I will sing unto the Lord for He has dealt bountifully with me ...*"[40] I affirmed the words. The Lord had dealt bountifully with me.

I messaged people to pray for me and phoned Doctor Abba to cancel the antibody injections. He sent an antiviral script to my chemist. While Peter was out getting the Paxlovid, I noticed there were hairs on my clothing. I counted ten! I'd read that covid and high fevers could cause one's hair to fall out. It made me chuckle. God, who knows the number of hairs on our head, would have to recount mine![41]

By the following morning, the convulsions had stopped. I had been taking Panadol and that brought my temperatures down for a while. When the Panadol wore off the fever came back.

That night the Holy Spirit said, *"It will soon be over."*

I woke the following morning with no fever. I still had pains and coughing but reminded myself it would soon be over.

The rash became very itchy and large hive-like lumps appeared, so I sent my GP a photo of the biggest one. We had a teleconference on the 26th July.

My GP thought it looked like hives too. "An allergic reaction, from being unwell" she said. "Get plenty of rest."

I had been.

"And take an antihistamine."

---

[40] Anonymous, found in several books, based on Psalm 13:6.
[41] Luke 12:7

I'm allergic to many of them but decided to try Clarityne. I only took one. Praise God it was okay.

On the 9th August, I asked the Holy Spirit what to do about the cough I still had 4 weeks after Covid.

"*Salt water,*" He said.

So, I began gargling with it and taking a couple of sips so it would wash my throat. I didn't cough that night and felt a lot better the following morning.

I continued reminding myself of what the Holy Spirit said, "*It will be over soon.*" It was -in the long scheme of things. I coughed for about 6 weeks which felt like forever at the time, and I was tired for some time after, but I was well enough to have my regular colonoscopy and gastroscopy on 22nd September.

A miracle? Three years before, after my last colonoscopy and gastroscope the surgeon said my stomach was full of polyps. Now there were none. The report said, "*Normal stomach.*"

Did the chemo kill them? Had my lactose free diet done it or was it a miracle? Whatever happened I was glad they'd gone. A few biopsies were done, which showed some angio dysplastic lesions in the right bowl and diverticulitis, but no adenomas or polyps.

My appointment with a neurologist was on the 6th September. I arrived on the right day but the wrong time. Amazingly, someone had just phoned to cancel their appointment when I arrived, so I still got in. Praise God! I'd waited since May for an appointment and felt as though that was long enough!

"No nasties," the neurologist said. Looking at my most recent scan, she confirmed the meningioma and pointed it out to me. It had been reported in a scan, but no one had pointed it out. She didn't think it was causing the problems

I'd been having. She thought they could be from the diabetes or unusual thyroid readings. Two years later when I went onto a continuous blood sugar monitor, I discovered if my sugars went too high, I'd be dizzy the following day. The dizziness would sometimes last a week. So, perhaps the neurologist was right in thinking it may have been caused by diabetes.

There was some good news. Although I had a poor memory, there was no sign of Alzheimer's. I still had a normal lot of brain for my age!

The neurologist suggested I have another brain scan in March and a nerve ending test. She said she'd speak with my haematologist to see if there was anything he thought was causing the balance issues etc. She gave me a referral to a physiotherapist for balance exercises.

I thought it would be a good idea to see a neurosurgeon as I'd eventually have to see one if the meningioma kept growing. They usually did. So, she made a referral to one as well, although she didn't think I needed to go under the knife. She was right. The neurosurgeon also said I didn't need regular visits. My GP could do three yearly scans, if needed.

Chapter 14 ✺ Power Perfected In Weakness

Knitting for our first grandchild, while gallery sitting at the Creative Hearts Art gallery in Australia Fair (2020)

Out of the blue the presence of the Lord came upon me, and I heard the words, "*Aimee is pregnant with a girl.*"

Aimee is one of our daughters, so I bought some baby girl outfits. The word proved true. Around that time, she conceived a girl.

Some weeks later, I had a dream about a tiny wriggly baby girl in my hand. She was about an inch long. This dream proved to be true too. She was a very wiggly baby in the womb and out. She wiggled so much they couldn't get a good scan of her. Her brother hadn't been like that.

I started knitting again. However, it wasn't as easy as it used to be. I kept losing my concentration and forgetting what stitches I was up to. I spent more time unpicking than knitting. I hadn't had these problems knitting for Harry, our first grandchild who'd been born about 18 months earlier. However, I persevered and eventually managed to complete some outfits.

I use a doll to model my knitting

In August 2022, I was reading how Sarah-Jane Biggara had asked the Lord if there were any doorways in the spirit that needed closing or opening.[42] So, I asked the Lord to show me any spiritual doors in the room I was in. I had a vision of the corner of a room. The floor was shining but there was a dark hole in one of the walls. So, I declared it closed and sealed in the name of Jesus. Then I saw another door above, and rays of light were shining down.

I heard the Lord say, "*Come up,*" and in the vision I went up above the clouds. I stood before a carpet of silver white clouds, shaped like balls of wool. I'd never seen or heard of mammatus clouds before, so they looked completely amazing and very strange.

That night I woke full of joy. I experienced a healing, and, in the morning, the Lord woke me with the words, "*I am bringing grace into your home.*" That was intriguing.

During the day, as I was praying in the same room where the hole had been, I suddenly saw flowers where the dark hole had been.

---

[42] (Biggart, 2021)

The following month, I was sitting with the Lord and had a vision of a rose. I love roses. To me they are perfectly beautiful. I didn't think much about the rose vision at the time until I heard the Holy Spirit whisper, *"Made perfect in weakness."*

I couldn't remember the first part of the verse, so I looked it up and concentrated on what I'd heard rather than seen, *"Power is perfected in weakness."*[43]

A large lump appeared in my groin, and an itchy rash on my stomach, so back I went to the doctor. She gave me a referral for another blood test and an ultrasound.

When I got home that day, I remembered the first part of the verse. *"My grace is sufficient for you."*

I was looking forward to the grace. I didn't know I'd have more years of one thing after another that would need it, including two more bouts of covid which would cause my blood sugars to skyrocket. I also had many infections. One bout meant I was on antibiotics for seven months.

I began feeling unwell and ended up with a boil just before Christmas. I'd had some in March. I went to see my GP. I didn't even notice her taking my temperature. I had a low-grade fever I hadn't noticed either. She gave me an antibiotic.

For about three years after the chemo, we tried many different tablets for diabetes with terrible side effects. I ended up on insulin because my blood sugars didn't go back down after covid. I also had very high blood pressure; one was 242/133. I was given different blood

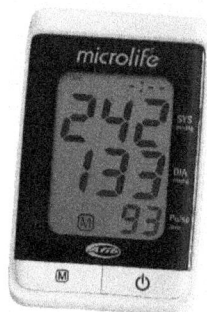

---

[43] 2 Corinthians 12:9

pressure tablets which also didn't agree with me. One made my blood pressure drop too much.

I went back to the neurologist who said my symptoms like dizziness, vomiting, throbbing in the ear and low level but long periods of pain were migraine. I told her I didn't get migraines. I'd had migraines when I was young but hadn't had one since I started having children. She told me I had silent migraines. This kind didn't have the strong headache pain. She gave me Sandomigran for all the symptoms I'd been having. However instead of preventing them, it triggered them.

The first one started with a phantom smell. I began smelling something like stale sandalwood, which was a phantom smell because I still had anosmia. Then two days later, on September the 18th 2023, I was lying on the couch watching television but had to stop as I couldn't concentrate, and my eyes were blurry. I thought I'd try reading, but I couldn't read the words. Then I noticed a circular, swirling whitish area moving across and around my vision. I blinked thinking there was something in my eye, but it didn't go away. Suddenly it looked like my eye lenses had cracked. It was like looking through jagged shards of glass. Then I was blind and couldn't see anything. I panicked and was told by the online health nurse to go to hospital.

In hospital, various tests were done. My blood pressure was high again. It was 206/99. I was given a magnesium infusion via drip. Then my speech became intermittently slurry, and I couldn't raise my right leg, so I was triaged to another hospital. They thought I was having a stroke or hemiplegic migraine.

I was placed in a single room and the man, doctor or nurse, I'm not sure, sent the nurses away and told them to close the door. They were busy.

He began the stroke spoon test by giving me something to drink from a spoon. I took one sip and lost consciousness. As I was coming round, I was surprised. He was still putting the spoon into my mouth. I couldn't move my teeth, so the spoon was scraping through them. I couldn't swallow either. Shortly later I was able to open my eyes.

"Now you look better," he said.

"Why?"

He didn't answer.

"Was I pale?" I asked.

He paused. "Yes," he said.

Later I wished I'd told him what happened, but right then I was in no condition to talk.

Suddenly he said, "I don't want you here by yourself." He wanted me where he could "keep a closer eye on me." So, he proceeded to have me moved to the room opposite the ward reception area.

I wasn't pleased about sharing a room. But then another strange thing happened. The man in the bed next to me was snoring very loudly. It sounded like a dragon roar. Suddenly I felt terrified. I kept crying out to God for help. I also sent a quick message to church leaders for prayer.

I didn't sleep. I was still awake at 6am when Helen, a friend from church and wife of our prayer leader Len, messaged me. She asked our heavenly father to have an angel with a flaming sword watching over me. That sounded good.

In the afternoon the symptoms had resolved so I went home. The diagnosis was aura with hemiplegic migraine or possibly a small stroke. The following day I developed another boil that needed an antibiotic, so back I went to my GP.

A month later I stopped taking the Sandomigran. I began experiencing a lot of episodes of fibrillation where momentarily I couldn't breathe. Normally I had only one in a day, but now it was more like one every hour. Two days later I had an out of body experience, only I was in my belly looking up. My body was unconscious, and an angel was doing something to my chest. Then as it left, I thought it was stroking me as though I was a pet cat. I also thought I caught a glimpse of Jesus behind the angel. There was so much love around the angel, only I was afraid. I didn't know what it was doing and why. Was it an angel from God or not?

As I thought about it the Holy Spirit said, "*Vigorous.*"

The angel had been doing a vigorous movement to my chest. I knew I'd been unconscious but had no memory of how I got that way.

That night and the next I woke, and my sleep seemed very pleasant to me. I had more mental energy than I'd had for a long time. I'd recently read the scripture about Jesus being strengthened by an angel. I was too and Helen's prayer was answered, although I didn't literally see the flaming sword.

It took a few days of thinking about it for me to realise the angel must have been doing CPR on my chest. Anyway, the fruit of its actions was that I was strengthened. In my weakness, I'd experienced God's power.

In November my sister Susan arrived. It was perfect timing. She also turned out to be a gift of grace during my weakness. I had finally gained the confidence to cut down a large tree branch, but instead of falling forward, it suddenly slid backwards. I didn't have time to get out of the way. The branch hit me in the groin and pushed me over. I landed on my lower back. The branch scraped down my leg and pinned me there.

The pain was so intense I thought my leg had been broken and pulled out of its socket. I

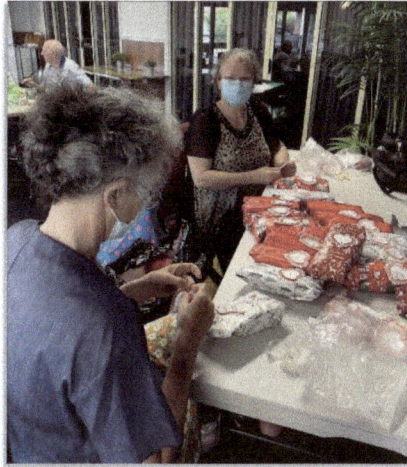

My sister Susan and me attaching the tags I'd made to the Christmas Angels presents

cried out to God. I didn't want a broken leg. Suddenly everything was filled with light.

I was lying on the bank. The chainsaw had been flung out of my hand and was still going. I just lay there. I couldn't move. The pain was shocking. Finally, I was able to move and saw Peter standing in front of the tree. He got the pair of crutches we had and took me to the Nerang Medical centre.

The doctor I saw, said I had a haematoma. He gave me antibiotic cream for the burns. He didn't think it was broken but told me to return if the pain became unbearable.

It *was* unbearable. I couldn't bear even the slightest touch. How was I going to rub the cream in?

Back home, the three of us prayed, and the hematoma disappeared overnight. We prayed again the following day, and I was able to touch my shin without severe pain.

I was so thankful to have Susan with us as I could only limp and hobble with the crutches. My hip and lower back were sore as well.

Susan cleaned, cooked and did some gardening. It was a real blessing. She even came with me to church where

Our wedding day

we attach the tags I'd made onto the 200 presents for the Christmas Angels hampers. Because she was with us, I started making the tags for the following year and was glad of her help.

In November, I was woken on our wedding anniversary with multiple visions of the sun bursting through clouds. I wondered what the Lord was saying.

Later in the day I was looking at a photo of my wedding gown and laughed. I'd screen printed and embroidered a sun burst on the bodice. God knew it was our anniversary and had given me the desire of my heart.

Sunshine, blue skies and flowers were the things I'd wanted for our marriage, so I'd depicted them on my gown. It symbolized happiness and good times. When I made the gown, I didn't know it was unrealistic, because life isn't like that. We need the rain too. However, the sun bursting through clouds is a wonderful symbol of hope and happiness even in adverse situations. You could say it is one of my life themes. The Son of God, like sunshine, is always bursting through the cloudy times. Power in weakness could also be the theme of my chemo journey.

Although I was still trying to find a medication for blood pressure and diabetes that didn't have adverse side-effects, I

Our three children at the beach house

was able to fly with Peter to New South Wales for a Christmas holiday. It was the first time in many years all our children were able to join us.

When I was younger, I'd had an image in my mind of what I'd like to do when I retired. I imagined a house by the beach with a window seat where I could sit and read. The thought came with a holiday feeling. The beach house we rented was in Catherine Bay. It had the same atmosphere of that mental image.

I went for walks along the beach and breathed in the beauty. I took many photos of the waves for a future painting, and it felt like that long ago desire had come to pass, even though I didn't do much reading with a toddler to entertain and family around me

Harry and his father at the beach house

135

and there wasn't a window seat.

The following month a friend from church came to visit. Her neighbour had given her flowers to give to someone who went to our church and deserved them. She immediately thought of me and told her neighbour about me. She didn't know roses and lilies were my favourite flowers and I love the look of wheat, so it felt like God who knows me intimately, had inspired the gift.

My weakness had been an opportunity for God to demonstrate His power again by inspiring a perfect gift. Just like the vision of a rose it was a perfect gift of grace.

A gift of flowers (2023)

Chapter 15 ◈ Hedge of protection

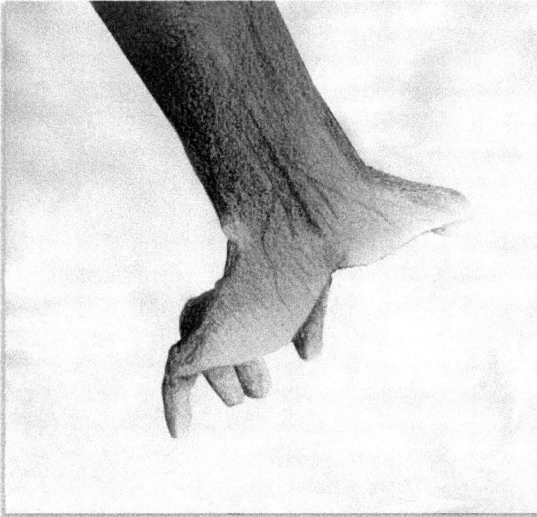

I made this image by taking the hand from "Hear My Cry" (1974)

Sometimes God shows us His hand is strong to help us go through a difficult thing, and sometimes He shows us His hand is strong to deliver us out of trouble, and sometimes He protects us, so we avoid a hard path.

I do like the testimonies that can come from trials and tribulations, but who doesn't prefer to avoid them? I was more than glad He sent the angel with healing for one of the biggest lymph nodes, at the beginning of my chemo journey. It meant I didn't have to go through the concomitant leg pain as well as the chemo side effects. I avoided that battle.

Another time I didn't even have to see the battle. I didn't even know what it was about! I woke from a night-time sleep and just saw the evidence. There were black and white feathers on the floor outside our bedroom door. They looked like the wing feathers of a black bird and a white bird. I asked Peter if he'd put them there.

"No," he said.

Was it a battle between a white and black angel during the night? I thought it must've been. It seemed to me God had arranged for the feathers to be there to remind me He was protecting us even while we slept. I thanked Him for doing so.

This wasn't the first time God had used feathers to remind me of His protection. In 2022 I'd woken hearing the words, "*I have covered thee*." They were coming out of my mouth like a breath of wind. I knew the Hebrew word for the Holy Spirit was *ruach* which meant "breath" and "wind," but why did He use the word "thee?" Was it so I'd take note of it? It did make me stop and think. Maybe it was like the burning bush that caught Moses attention, or honey in the lion carcass that stopped Samson in his tracks.[44]

I also wondered why it was coming out of my mouth. Then the Holy Spirit reminded me of the song we used to sing in the 70's.[45] It used the words of scripture, "*The word of God is near thee even in thy mouth*."[46] God was speaking through me and confirming the word that came out of my mouth. He had *covered* me.

Later that day I just happened to read an email with a testimony about feathers appearing around a person. They quoted Psalm 91:4 which I've translated as, "*With His feathers He will overshadow you*." Again, God was confirming the word that came from my mouth. He would protect,

---

[44] Exodus 3, Judges 14:8
[45] Adapted from (Vale, 1971)
[46] Romans 10:8

hedge, cover and even screen me. He would block that which would harm me.[47]

22/2/22

The following day while sitting in my prayer/reading chair, I felt something poking me in the back. I thought it must be a Farmer's Friend seed and pulled at it.[48] It was stuck in my clothing. When I finally got it out, I saw it wasn't a seed but a small white feather. I thanked the Lord for poking me in the back. I needed His reminder. I also thanked Him for manifestations of feathers. This one reminded me He was my refuge and protection.

On the 22/2/22 when I woke, I found two white feathers on my bedroom floor. The date being all twos was interesting, especially since there were exactly two feathers that time. There were no feathers in our bedding. It wasn't a coincidence, but a God incident. God got my attention. It was another reminder He was protecting me.

In October of 2022 I started a new diabetic medication in addition to the one I was already on. It had been lowering my blood sugars but making me very tired with sweating and what felt like very low sugars in the night. Early on the 28th I was dreaming about groups of children and teachers who were all busy doing activities. Then one group started serving cake. I kept thinking, "What is the message?" Then I heard a voice say, "The message is, get up and eat." It

---

[47] (Harris et al., 1980) p.623
[48] Bidens Pilosa also known as Cobbler's Peg (Brisbane City Council, 2025).

reminded me of the angel who woke Elijah and said the same thing to Him.[49]

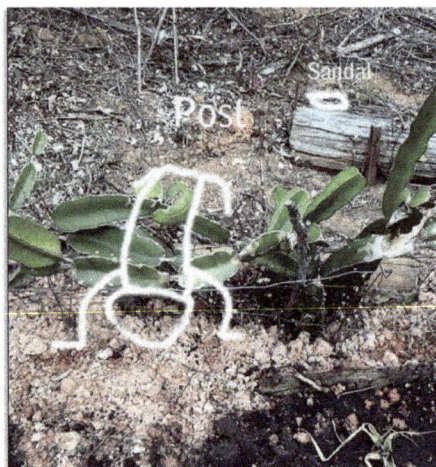
Gymnastics miracle (2023)

I woke from the dream and knew that message was for me. My sugars were too low. I needed to get up and eat. I was tired and just wanted to go back to sleep but obeyed. God was protecting me from a hypo.

God isn't limited in how He protects. He does it in many ways. In 2023, I had my back to the dragon fruit plant and was pulling out a stake. It broke and I ended up falling. Miraculously, instead of falling backwards down the bank, suddenly I was flipped over and landed on my hands and feet facing the opposite direction straddling the prickly plant. No part of my body was touching it. My back was arched up over it and my face looking down!

I couldn't move from that position for some time as I didn't want to be pricked. When I checked the plant afterwards, a piece of the plant was bent back towards me. If my body had broken it, it would've bent forward, not back towards me. That was strange. I praised God!

My toes hurt as one sandal got caught on a metal stake and came off, but there were no marks on my bare toes. They could've been torn by the metal. My sandal was caught

---

[49] 1 Kings 19:7

on the edge of the wood, but my toes hadn't touched it. How amazing. Again, I praised God for a gymnastic deliverance!

God's ability to protect is endless and far reaching. I hadn't thought about it being like a hedge until 2024 when I had a vision of a green hedge. The hedge was so long I couldn't see the end of it. It was also so thick I couldn't see through it. It was very straight, unusually so, and not thin like the hedges on our property. One can see through them.

In the vision, as I looked closely at the hedge, I could see the leaves were a bit prickly and mildly scary. It stood in front of a tree protecting it. I knew it was my tree and some kind of nut tree.

In real life, I have a Macadamia nut tree. The tree in my vision didn't look the same. Its branches were more compact, and its overall shape tended towards a triangle.

When I came out of the vision, I asked God about it. I knew what I'd seen was a hedge of protection. I knew it spoke of His protection which I could see was endless and far reaching and able to hide things. Nothing could penetrate what He protected, but why was the hedge protecting a nut tree? (Don't laugh!)

A few days later someone tried to use my credit card details to purchase something on the other side of the world. They didn't get anything because the bank immediately blocked them and contacted me.

I had the answer to my question. Why a tree with nuts on it? The nuts reminded me of the saying, to squirrel something away, like a squirrel storing nuts or someone saving money in a bank. God had protected my tiny store of monetary nuts.

The previous month, God had also protected a credit card -Peter's one. Our daughter had accidentally left it on the roof of the car. We went to the shops and discovered it was missing. On the way home, she searched the road through the car window and when we turned into our street, there it was. Right next to a water drainage hole. It could've fallen into the drain, but it just missed it. We were so thankful the credit card had been protected.

While editing this section in 2025, I remembered Helen's prayer for me. She'd prayed for an angel with a flaming sword to protect me. In the Biblical account, a flaming sword had been placed to *shamar* the way to the tree of life.[50] One of the meanings of this Hebrew word is to keep, or hedge about like an official or like a legal word.[51] Angelic beings called Cherubim had been placed with it. Their name has the idea of adoring God in it.[52] These two things, the word of God and adoration acted like a hedge of protection.

I asked the Lord for something to write to finish this chapter on protection. I didn't want an incident where I needed His protection, that would be too scary ... or would it?

I was on my way to a regular Friday prayer meeting, where we prayed for the city. I wanted to have God's heart for the people we prayed for, so I asked Him for it.

The answer came quickly. At the prayer meeting, as soon as I closed my eyes to pray, nearly the whole room was filled with thickness. I panicked. I thought it would completely squash me against the wall.

Suddenly I saw a white wall right in front of me. It seemed to be as tall as the room, and I no longer felt like I would be squashed. It was protecting me. The atmosphere between me and the wall was one of light and joy.

---

[50] Genesis 3:24, (Blair, 2014)
[51] (Harris et al., 1980) p.454
[52] (Harris et al., 1980) p918-9

I noticed a small hole in the wall. It looked just like the one on my kitchen wall. I'd removed two decorative plates from the wall and plastered over one of the screw holes. The other hole I'd left unfilled as I was thinking of putting a new picture hook in it.

The vision reminded me of Ephesians 4:10: *He who descended is the very One who ascended above all the heavens, in order to fill all things.* It also reminded me of the hedge vision I'd had a few weeks previously. It seemed to me God was saying He is in our midst as a protective wall. His desire is to fill all things so together we are also like a protective wall.

After seeing the wall, I heard the words, "*Song in the night.*" I immediately thought, "Yes, and light in the darkness." Our God is this good.

"*Dance,*" I heard Him say and I saw my spirit was dancing around the room. I didn't have the balance needed for my feet to follow, but I had joy in abundance. The protective wall made room for me, so much room that I could even dance. I let my arms dance.

Next, I saw Jesus in our midst. I couldn't put my finger on what His demeanour looked like. A waiter wasn't quite right. He was wearing a simple white gown. It was thick and soft—the character of sheep's wool. In His arms was a large empty bowl. At first, I thought it would be filled with bread for a meal, or water for washing feet. Was there anything in the bowl?

I looked again, staring hard into the bowl but it was empty, just dark inside. What was Jesus doing holding an empty bowl?

That night I woke with a song going through my mind. *Hallelujah, our God reigns.*[53] It was the song in the night. I

---

[53] (Johnson & Mackintosh, 2011)

was adoring God like the name of the angelic beings guarding the tree of life. The word I'd heard had come to pass!

The next two days, as I was meditating on all these things, I knew God was showing me what He is like. Although He is Lord of all, in our midst His manner is still like one who serves. He doesn't come to fill everything so there is no room for us, or to squash us like the thickness I felt at first. His protection makes room for us.

And what about the empty bowl in Jesus' arms? The bowl represented a person, such as one who hadn't been filled with the Spirit of God. God cares for them too. He has plans for them, even for criminals. He sees their potential, like the empty hole in my wall. His ultimate desire is to fill them so they too can be useful and part of His protective wall. Then I realised what His demeanour in the vision was like. It was like a mother patiently holding her baby in her arms.

So, with that attitude I blessed the Gold Coast city. I said, "God's desire is for you. Be filled with all the good things God has for you. May your people come to know Him as their hedge of protection and become one too."

A few days later, at an Australian Prophetic Intercessors meeting we were asked to bless the person on our left. The person who blessed me, declared a Biblical blessing on me *"You will be blessed when you come in and blessed when you go out."*[54]

The following morning, on the way out, I declared that blessing and prayed for protection. As I drove along the highway, I was nearly squashed between two cars because the car in front slowed very quickly and the car behind was

---

[54] Deuteronomy 28

a little close. Again, the enemy wanted to squash me, but God protected me.

Even though God holds us in His arms, whether we are filled or not, we can still experience suffering. Jesus suffered and so did His disciples. The apostle Paul was beaten and whipped, stoned, shipwrecked, and in many perilous situations. He was often hungry, thirsty, cold and naked.[55] In heaven there will be no tears of sorrow or pain, but here on earth we still experience some. God is able to deliver me, but if He has other plans, I will still pray for that hedge of protection and adore Him.

In January 2025, just after Bruce, our church leader had preached a sermon about faith, obedience and courage, I had a vision. It had a similar message. I saw a small tree lusciously covered in strong dark leaves. Around it on all sides except the front, was something like a rock and a cloud.

"Is it a rock or a cloud?" I asked the Lord.

"*Both*," He replied.

God is both rock and cloud and he'd been both to me through my chemo journey.

Two days later I remembered how, in the vision, the rock had changed. At first it was definitely rock, but as I continued looking it was more like cloud. Right at the end it looked like a puffy keto breakfast hot pocket, puffing up in a frypan. As I thought about this shape the words, "*air bag*" came into my mind. Yes! That's what it also looked like—an airbag protecting a tree.

Having been in five serious car accidents, an airbag had special meaning for me. Only one of the cars I was in had an airbag and that one had failed to work during the accident.

---

[55] 2 Corinthians 11:24-27

Yet I am still here because God has the protecting and cushioning power of an airbag!

On the 22nd June 2025, while worshiping God in church, I had a vision of God's hand coming down. I felt His affirmation. I searched for Bible verses with hand in them and Psalm 139:5 said what I saw and felt. *"Behind and before you hedge me and place your hand upon me."*

Even though I had God's protection and unlimited resources, like the coloured boxes I'd seen in the spiritual realm when the angel came with healing from God,[56] chemo was one thing I still had to face *head on.* However, because of the grace of God, I didn't have to do it by myself. I had God's hand, Church, family, friends, doctors, nurses, navigators and hospital staff helping me. They were all like wonders to me.

---

[56] Page 32

Chapter 16 ❧ Abundant Life

Trumpeting Abundance (2021)

All the health issues I had following cancer left a mark on me, like the little hole that was left in our kitchen wall after I removed a picture screw. Sickness can often cause us to focus on ourselves and worry about our health. This happened to me. I was often my focus. But God is patient and His love abundant. His desire was to fill that hole.

I'd started going out again and when I did, I wore my mask even though people sometimes made negative comments about it. Some even coughed at me, but it didn't stop me from wearing it. I believed it gave me some protection as I was still immunocompromised.

In February 2023 Len had organised a prayer retreat at the House of Prayer in Carrara. I'd recovered from a second bout of Covid at Christmas and was well enough, so I went wearing my mask.

We began by worshiping God in song and as we did, I saw brown ribbons released into the air above me. Apart from the colour, they looked just like the ribbons I danced with in church from time to time. They also looked like the ribbons I painted in artworks and reminded me of a previous vision of my coloured ribbons being released above me.[57] At that time, the Holy Spirit was saying to let go of the painting I was working on. It depicted a glass jar with ribbons. God wanted me to paint a volcano with ribbons, from a high perspective, not a low one.

Unfinished artwork of glass jar with ribbons (2019)

Now, in an instance I was set free from my health worries. Like the ribbons, they were released into the air above me. I felt so free and full of joy. It was abundant life flowing out from me like ribbons.

---

[57] *A High Perspective* can be seen on page 123.

Len had organised the first day into three sessions. The first was on grace, the next love and the third, fellowship.

For the session on love, we meditated on 2 Corinthians 13:11-14, and I had a vision of an eye. A waterfall came from it. The water was so pure. It was clean and shining. Then a hand placed a single tear drop on top of the waterfall and held it there.

It seemed like God was saying, where we have one tear, God's is a waterfall beneath ours. I knew what that was like. When my children were little and hurt themselves, sometimes I cried more than they did.

I thought about Jesus weeping.[58] Like a mother hen His desire was and still is to gather us under His wings. He adores us.

While editing this in 2025, I heard a song I used to listen to in the '80's.

And Jesus said, come to the waters stand by my side, I know you are thirsty, you won't be denied. I felt every tear drop when in darkness you cried, and I strove to remind you that for those tears I died.[59]

The following day I had a vision in church of shells on the sand. They looked as though they'd been squashed. They'd folded in on themselves. As I looked at them, I thought, if I were painting them, I'd need to add a bit of the scallop so others would know what kind of shell they were.

---

[58] Luke 11:35, Luke 19:41
[59] (Carter et al., 1971)

In some countries, scallop shells are worn by pilgrims as a sign of who they are. So later I made a quick watercolour sketch and added a bit of the scallop.

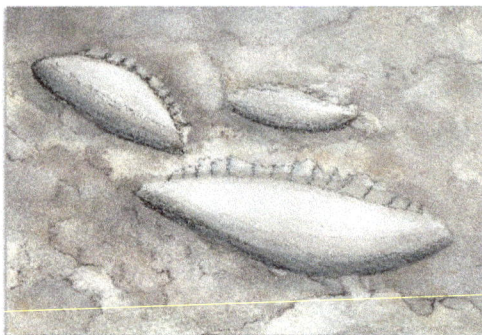

In the vision, I saw a flash of brilliant white and knew Jesus' feet were on the sand near the shells. It was a similar message to the song. Jesus knows what we go through and sometimes it's hard. The cross wasn't easy for Him either, but our tears were one of the reasons He endured it.

In the Bible, David, also had times where he cried, even though he was very courageous and slew a giant when he was young. He said God put his tears in a bottle and recorded it in His book.[60] So we know our tears are not dismissed.

That Sunday, I shared a *God sees you and knows what it's like to be human* message in church and afterwards a lady told me the message was for her. She'd asked God if He saw her. A man also indicated he had anguish in his soul from a difficult path. I'd seen at least three shells in the vision and prayed for them all that they'd receive God's comfort and help.

At the prayer retreat, during the session on Fellowship, I heard the Lord say, "*Fellowship is like a garden.*"

I thought about how gardens need tending and so do relationships. I thought of the more painful processes like pruning. Fruit trees that are pruned tend to grow more

---

[60] Psalm 56:8

vigorously and bear more fruit. This kind of tending doesn't sound pleasant to our wayward natures. Sometimes painful experiences prune us. We cannot avoid all troubles on earth, but they can be used for our good. Imagine a pain free life. If that were so, would we ever know the saving, healing and protecting side of God, or his tender heart? Would we experience His tears or think we were self-sufficient and didn't need Him.

In 1995 I published a poem about what we call the fruit of the Spirit.[61] Here are two verses from it.[62]

> *Some fruit need a winter*
> *that is wet and cold.*
> *Some fruit are rare*
> *more precious than gold.*
>
> *Patience needs time*
> *long-suffering, pain*
> *And forgiveness comes*
> *when the giver is slain.*

In other words, even if we are filled with God's Spirit, some fruit cannot be produced apart from suffering. Although I hate pain and suffering, I know if we allow Him to, He will work everything for good and sometimes we experience the miraculous when He intervenes and heals us.[63]

I saw some of the good He brought from my cancer journey. For example, I spent a lot more time clinging to

---

[61] Galatians 5:22-23

[62] (Phillips, 1995)

[63] Romans 8:28

Him and as a result, have even more testimonies of His abundance, the abundance of His love, His help and grace.

In 2025 I thought, no matter how difficult a thing is, we too can work all things for good.

The second day of the retreat, I was in the Spirit and experienced an angel placing a cloak around my shoulders. Len said it was a cloak of protection. Someone asked me what colour it was. I didn't have the language on hand to speak about it. After meditation I found this language: The cloak and the angel were spirit, kind of see-through, like moving air, yet somehow solid as I could see the shape. The cloak looked like it was made of tiny bits of light.

There were other wonderful experiences at the retreat. I heard the Lord say, *"Come and see,"* and I was immediately in a very spacious place above the earth and the clouds. There, I perceived the endlessness of His resources.

It wasn't the first nor the last time He showed me the abundance of His resources. As I said before, right at the beginning of my cancer journey, He'd let me see a wall of pastel-coloured box-like drawers that were available to the angel He sent with healing for me. He showed me these pastel drawers again some years later during our Friday prayer group. I'd experienced it too, on the 15th of November 2020, while worshiping the Lord in church. I had a vision of water pouring from a grand cloud that went right up one side of my vision. I felt the abundance of God. The abundance wasn't in the shapes or things I saw in the vision. It was in the presence of His Spirit. I could feel it.

After church I went to my friend Paula's place. I was telling her about the vision and the Holy Spirit pointed out a Bible verse on her table: *"All the paths of the Lord drip with abundance."*[64] That includes hard paths. My cancer journey was one of those.

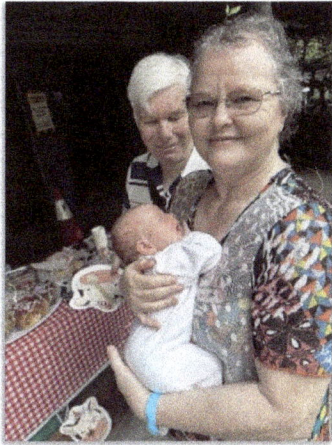

Peter and me with Zara, our second grandchild

I left Paula's place and at home, began painting the artwork *Trumpeting Abundance.*[65] I hope that's what I've done in this book, and you have caught a glimpse of God's abundant love too.

It is amazing, but the message on my calendar for the month I was editing this section was, *"Even the hard pathways overflow with abundance."* I checked my reference and found I'd written the wrong chapter so was able to correct it.

Another wonderful thing happened at the retreat. When I was back in my chair after perceiving God's endless resources, I heard the Lord say, *"I turn the page of your life over."*

It did seem like I'd turned a corner. The following month I was well enough to fly again, so Peter and I were able to go to Sydney and celebrate our grandson's birthday and see our new granddaughter. She was a fulfillment of a promise from the Lord that I'd live to see my grandchildren, and so I have. God did indeed lead me *through* the chemo. It felt like I was out the other side and on a new page too.

---

[64] Psalm 65:11
[65] Page 147

Postscript

In June 2025, I heard a very angelic voice say, "*Cancer.*" I wondered if I was going to have to go through cancer and chemo again. However, the following day I met someone with cancer, so I prayed for her.

A month later I had a vivid dream. My pet cat was going around the circuit again, only the terrain had changed this time. It walked steadily with its tail high. As it walked, the water went over its head, but it kept on walking steadily towards a city that rose up out of the water. A voice said to me, "*You are the best thing for her.*"

Being diagnosed with cancer a second time would be deep waters, a very hard path. So, I interceded for those who were facing another round after being in remission. Having been through cancer once I had more empathy for others on a similar path and could pray more knowledgeably.

I went back to bed and had visions of a lioness and a lot of different cats. Yes, there are many who face cancer more than once. Our bodies are not going to last forever, even if God heals us from time to time.

If you are suffering don't lose hope. If you are about to go around the mountain or circuit again, don't let disappointment lead your thoughts, instead, fix your eyes on Jesus. Like the ancient ones we have wonders to look forward to, including a pain-free body and a place in a city Jesus went before us to prepare.[66]

---

[66] Hebrews 11, John 14:3-4

My artworks for the New Hope Charity Fundraiser

Pet Scan Report 28/8/21

FDG PET CT STUDY

CLINICAL HISTORY
Stage III (at least) lymphoma

TECHNIQUE
Following IV administration of 290MBq F-18 FDG emission tomographic images
of the body were acquired from the vertex to thigh. Low dose noncontrast CT
was performed for attenuation correction and anatomic correlation. The
blood glucose level was 6.2mmol-L.

FINDINGS
Mediastinal blood pool SUV max 1.7
Splenic uptake SUV max 2.2
Hepatic uptake SUV max 2.5

Head/Neck:
FDG distribution throughout the head and neck appears physiological. No FDG
avid or enlarged cervical or supraclavicular lymph nodes are identified. No
large space-occupying lesion on the low-dose noncontrast CT brain.

Thorax:
Moderate FDG avidity is identified within a small para-oesophageal lymph
node measuring 11 x 9 mm (SUV max 4.4) and within a left retrocrural lymph
node measuring 15 x 12 mm (SUV max 6.9). No further FDG avid or enlarged
mediastinal, hilar or axillary lymph nodes are identified. No pulmonary
nodules are identified. No pleural or pericardial effusion.

Abdomen:
Intense FDG avidity is identified within the large retroperitoneal
lymphadenopathy with the largest node in the aorto caval position measuring
55 x 37 x 121 mm (SUV max 13.4). There are further surrounding FDG avid
retroperitoneal lymph nodes also identified. A further larger node in the
left lower para-aortic region measures 41 x 39 x 65 mm (SUV max 11.8).
Central necrosis is demonstrated within some of the lymph nodes. There are
also bilateral FDG avid common iliac lymph nodes. Within the pelvis there
are FDG avid enlarged left external iliac lymph nodes and left inguinal
lymph nodes also identified. A left external iliac node measures 17 x 14 mm
(SUV max 9.4) and a the large left inguinal node measures 34 x 26 mm (SUV
max 11.1).

The spleen appears normal in size and FDG avidity. The cranial caudal
dimension measures 10.5 cm. No FDG avid splenic lesions are identified. No
FDG avid hepatic lesions. Previous cholecystectomy is noted. Within the
limitations of a noncontrast CT the remainder of the solid abdominal viscera
appear normal. The bowel has a normal CT appearance. No free fluid.

Musculoskeletal:
No focal FDG avid osseous lesions are identified. There is low grade
diffuse activity identified throughout the bone marrow. Degenerative uptake
is evident at the shoulder joints, AC joints, SC joints and both hip joints.

COMMENT
FDG avid nodal disease is demonstrated both above and below the diaphragm
with bulky retroperitoneal disease.

No extra nodal, splenic or osseous involvement is identified.

Note: SUV greater than 2.5 is indicative of cancer, although less than 2.5 can be cancerous too.

Notice on my hospital room door

PINDARA
PRIVATE HOSPITAL

CHEMOTHERAPY PRECAUTIONS
FOR PATIENTS AND THEIR VISITORS

Doctors and Nurses in the hospital know how to protect themselves from Chemotherapy. You will need to take some precautions to protect your family, friends and other visitors. You should use these precautions whether you are at home or in hospital for seven days after your chemo (unless advised differently by a healthcare professional). Your bodily fluids urine, faeces, vomit are all potentially damaging to your friends and family, so you need to protect them by following some simple rules.

- **Flush the toilet twice after each use** – Do this regardless of whether you passed urine or faeces. If at home use a separate toilet to everyone else (if possible). In hospital **DO NOT** allow visitors to use your toilet.

- If you vomit into the toilet, make sure you flush it twice making sure you wipe around the edges to clean any splashes. If you vomit into a bowl or bucket, flush vomit into the toilet, double flush and clean receptacle with hot soapy water. Dry with disposable paper towel and throw away immediately after use. Do not use a regular tea towel or dish cloth.

- Whilst you are in hospital, please allow the staff to help you, and remind your visitors to avoid your body fluids (Urine, Faeces, Vomit etc.).

What happens if someone accidently comes into contact with my bodily fluids?
Don't panic! Have the person wash the area with warm soapy water. Repeat several times. If necessary they can even take a shower. A single exposure should not have any lasting effects, but they should avoid any further exposures.

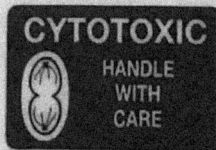

CYTOTOXIC
HANDLE
WITH
CARE

References

Biggart, S.-J. (2021). *Seeing Beyond: how to make supernatural sight your daily reality*. Destiny Image Publishers, INC.

Blair, T. (Ed.). (2014). *The Hebrew - English Interlinear ESV Old Testament*. Crossway.

Carter, M., Jacobs, P., Carter, W., & Stevens, R. (1971). For Those Tears I died. On *Come to the waters*. Maranatha Music.

Crocker, M., Houston, J., & Lightelm, S. (2013). Oceans (Where my feet may fail). On *Zion*. Hillsong United.

Harris, R. L., Archer, G. L., & Walke, B. K. (1980). *Theological Workbook of the Old Testament*. Moody Publishers.

Johnson, J., & Mackintosh, I. (2011). God I Look To you. On *Be Lifted High*. Bethel Music.

Lake, B., Johnson, J., & Carnes, K. J. (2021). Send Me. Bethel Music.

Litt, A. M. D. (Ed.). (1968). *The R.S.V. Interlinear Greek - English New Testament*. Samuel Bagster And Sons Limited.

Neusch, S. (2021). I Am Releasing the Grace Keys! . *Elijah List*.

Phillips, J. (2012). *Word Power Poetry & Poetics: visual digital & concrete* Wing To Wing.

Phillips, J. K. (1995). *In Their Likeness*. P. J. Phillips Consultants Ltd.

Stevens, J., Hesler, J., Hesler, M., & Skaggs, M. (2019). Raise A Hallelujah. On *Victory*. Bethel Music.

Vale, A. (1971). Joy Of The Lord. The Joy of the Lord Publishing Co.

Author Bio

Jennifer Kathleen Phillips
GradDipTh, BEd, DipIT, TTC, DipTchg

Jennifer Phillips is an award-winning Christian author. You may want to read her first memoir called "I Want To Travel With You." She has been a member of many organisations including the Genesis Writing Group, the Gold Coast Writers Association and the Australian Federation of Graduate Women where she also did a term as president. She was a teacher and developed courses, including a successful early reading program. She taught all ages over her working life and as a lay preacher in the Methodist Church of NZ. She has received awards in a range of fields including the university title of Massey Scholar and The Victoria Gibbons Prize for academic excellence. She has authored books covering a range of subjects and genres and enjoys crafting for charities, holding card-making workshops, making prophetic art and regularly participating in prophetic intercession and sharing.

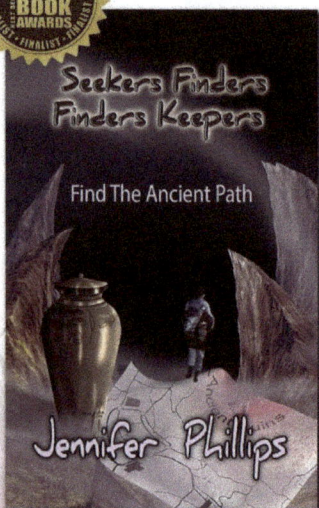

Find The Ancient Path

2020 Next Generation Indie Book Awards Finalist

After her mother dies, Haras is left with an important message for the father she has never known, but how will she ever find him? Did he go looking for the ancient path? Haras's quest leads her to discover treasure she never set out to find.

Suitable for Young adults and up.

It can be orderd through a range of book-stores including Koorong Bookstores, Amazon and Booktopia.
It is also available as a Kindle ebook.

http://jenniferphillips.com.au

www.ingramcontent.com/pod-product-compliance
Lightning Source LLC
Chambersburg PA
CBHW051246020426
42333CB00025B/3070